OUR CHARACTER, OUR FUTURE

OUR CHARACTER, OUR FUTURE

Reclaiming America's
Moral Destiny

ALAN KEYES

Edited by GEORGE GRANT

ZondervanPublishingHouse
Grand Rapids, Michigan

A Division of HarperCollinsPublishers

96 97 98 99 00 01 02 03 /❖ DH/ 10 9 8 7 6 5 4 3 2

CONTENTS

Part Three
Staking a Claim for Our Destiny

FOREWORD: HOW THIS BOOK CAME TO BE

G. K. Chesterton once quipped that "America is the only nation in the world that is founded on a creed." Other nations find their identity and cohesion in ethnicity, or geography, or cultural tradition. But America was founded on certain ideas—about freedom, about human dignity, about social responsibility. It was this profound peculiarity that most struck Alexis de Tocqueville during his famous visit to this land at the beginning of the nineteenth century. He called it "American exceptionalism."

In essence, this is the core of the message of Alan Keyes. Whether on the stump, in print, over the airwaves, or in animated one-on-one conversation, this remarkably eloquent spokesman for traditional mores is likely to remind his listeners that America's special blessings are the result of generations-long adherence to this special creed. They are also likely to hear him proclaim that if we are to overcome our current cultural woes, we will have to return to that adherence—and *post haste*.

The chapters that make up this book were gleaned from those speeches, articles, comments, and conversations. They were selected, edited, and revised amidst the mind-numbingly busy schedule that necessarily attends political campaigns these days.

Chapter 1 is a slightly revised version of Dr. Keyes' now famous Lincoln Day speech in New Hampshire. Broadcast repeatedly nationwide over C-Span's cable channels and Focus On the Family's radio network, it has come to epitomize his clarion cry for a return to those principles that first launched America's great experiment in liberty.

Chapter 2 is a transcription of a speech delivered to the Federalist Society's National Lawyers' Convention. It outlines his belief that genuine freedom relies upon the exercise of responsibility, discipline, and self-government.

Chapters 3 through 34 are slightly revised versions of Dr. Keyes' syndicated newspaper column. Covering a wide range of issues and concerns, they seek to apply his conception of *Declaration* principles to the practical affairs of everyday life.

Finally, chapter 35 contains a transcription of a powerful speech delivered to a meeting of Intercessors for America. In it, Dr. Keyes expresses his hope for the recapturing of America's special destiny through deep spiritual healing.

Taken together, this representative survey of Dr. Keyes' thought is offered in the hope that others will likewise sound the alarms—and that once again, America might be a nation of the creed.

George Grant

One

THE CASE
FOR CHARACTER

What sense is there in winning, in success, or even in prosperity if there is not truth? We really are reaching the point in this society where people are denying that there is any line to be drawn between truth and falsehood, right and wrong. But if that's the case, then our whole way of life can't work any more—because it is based on the sense that there are certain self-evident truths, that those self-evident truths support a certain idea of human justice, which requires respect for human rights, that, therefore, you must have elections and due process, and all the other things we consider to be the hallmarks of freedom. If there is no difference between right and wrong, then none of that is true, and there is no need to respect individual rights, there is no requirement that to be legitimate government has to be based upon consent, and the only thing that separates us from tyranny and despotism is that at the moment nobody has yet gained the upper hand.

1

THE MESSAGE OF FREEDOM

We don't have money problems. We have moral problems.

America has once again arrived at a momentous crossroads. We are going to have to decide—as we have had to decide so many times in the past—whether we shall only *speak* of justice and *speak* of principle or whether we shall *stand* and *fight* for them. We are going to have to decide whether we shall quote the words of the *Declaration of Independence* with real conviction or whether we shall take that document and throw it on the ash heap of history as we adopt the message of those who insist that we stand silent in the face of injustice.

When it comes to deciding whether we shall stand by the great principle that declares that all human beings are "created equal" and "endowed by their Creator" with the "right to life," it seems to me, there is no choice for silence.

Again, *there is no choice for silence.*

Thus, for instance, those so-called Conservatives who are recommending that we avoid the pro-life issue in our public discourse and civic responsibilities are actually recommending—as some people decided in the Whig Party, in the years before the Civil War, that they would be silent on the great issue of principle that faced this nation—we should be silent.

And you remember what happened to the Whigs—once the most powerful political force in America. They vanished altogether.

Modern cultural and political Conservatism grew up as a movement aimed first and foremost at dealing with that kind of moral irresponsibility—standing on the principle that Lincoln articulated: you cannot have the right to do what is wrong.

In the public arena, there are innumerable spokesmen clamoring for public attention today. Whether from the Right or the Left, the focus and crux of their message is basically the same. They talk about money. They talk about budgets, deficits, gross national products, and trade imbalances. "It's the economy, stupid," is their mantra.

But you and I both know, if we are willing to look ourselves in the eye, what the truth is. America's problems are *not* merely economic.

Why is it that we spend so much money dealing with welfare and illegitimacy? Why is it that we spend so much money dealing with crime and violence in our streets? Why is it that we even spend so much money dealing with the problems of irresponsible behaviors that contribute to the decline of the health of this nation? I think you know in your heart what the real answer is.

We don't have money problems. We have moral problems. And it is time we stood up and faced that truth.

But, I don't know how we're going to face that truth if, as has been so often suggested, we can look our daughters in the eye and tell them that it is somehow consistent with freedom for them to trample on the human rights of their unborn offspring.

We are going to have to find the courage one of these days to tell people that freedom is not an easy discipline. Freedom is not a choice for those who are lazy in their heart and in their respect for their own moral capacities.

Freedom requires that at the end of the day, we accept the constraint that is required, the respect for the laws of nature and nature's God that say unequivocally that our daughters do not have the right to do what is wrong, that our sons do not have the right to do what is wrong. We do not have the right to steal bread from the mouths of the innocent, we do not have the right to steal life from the womb of the unborn.

Some people may say that if we stand up and we speak out and we fight for this basic principle, we'll be dividing the nation and the burgeoning Conservative movement. But I don't think so. The Republican Party, for instance, was *born* on a clear commitment to principle. It was founded by those who had the courage to stand before the American people and in the face of the threat of a greater division than we'll ever face, insist that we had to respect the principles that make us great, the principles that make us strong, the principles that make us free.

Here we are more than a hundred years later and I'll tell you, we're going to have to do it again.

Look at what is happening in the streets of our cities. Look at what is happening to our families today. Do you think that the decline of marriage and the moral dissolution of the family is a money problem? Or do you think it is a problem that comes from putting the self first, from deciding that there are no obligations that have to be respected, and that at the end of the day freedom is just another kind of empty licentiousness?

We know better and our Founders knew better and it is time that we get back to the truth. The men and women who first launched the great experiment in liberty we enjoy to this day did not tell us that freedom would be an easy road. They offered us a hard-won vision of the future of America. It was not a vision of licentious freedom and stupid self-indulgence. Instead, it was a vision of freedom based upon the fear of God and the respect for law.

So why is it that out of the mouths of all our contemporary statesmen we hear all kinds of great emotional words, slogans, and sound bites—but not the simple truths that our Founders, from

Washington and Jefferson to Lincoln and all of their successors ,spoke right up until we got to our own cowardly times? Whatever became of the undiluted message of true freedom?

I talk about abortion not just because of the issue in and of itself, but because I think it epitomizes the deeper issue, which is the corruption of our idea of freedom—a corruption that is really killing us. I think abortion is a very dramatic example of that corruption and its consequences, because obviously that has direct consequences for the heart that we need to sustain the family. If we harden our hearts against our offspring, and if we aggrandize our self-fulfillment to the extent that we are even willing to kill our offspring, that is the extreme case of the self-centered and egotistical and self-worshipping concept of freedom I think is being promoted in various ways in the society.

We are not going to remain a free people if we insist on being a corrupt and licentious people. We are not going to remain a free people if we arrogate to ourselves the right to destroy the rights of others. And that is exactly what we are doing when we embrace the so-called "pro-choice" agenda—which is actually just the pro-abortion agenda.

I think it is empty to praise the courage of the men and women who have died in the service of this country's freedom and its principles and yet decide that we simply cannot muster the courage to stand up for them ourselves. Many or few—or even alone if we must—it is essential that we deny the legitimacy of that kind of compromise. It was moral courage that built America. That is the true foundation of freedom.

The vaunted American Dream was not, as some would have us believe, a dream of material progress and prosperity, and great cities suffused in mountains of money. Not at all. Economics is important, but in the long life of a nation, it is ultimately subordinate to the moral facts.

To be sure, I am glad that we have achieved that prosperity, even though it came at much expense to some of my forebears.

But even those who toiled in the depths of slavery, had an understanding of the real dream of American freedom.

It was and is the dream of moral dignity that comes from respecting our true moral capacity. It was and is the dream of self-government that comes from respecting the fact that in the end, freedom is not just a choice, it is not just an opportunity. It can be a burden and a sacrifice. And, above all, it is the obligation to respect the truth of our moral identity.

That moral identity can unite us across every line of race and color and creed, so long as we have the courage to stand for it.

And I think you know by now, looking at the overall dismal state of our culture, that if we abandon that line of principle, there is little hope left for America.

At every point in our history when we have had the choice between right and wrong, we have chosen in the end what is right. For that we can certainly be grateful. But, I believe we shall do it again. I believe we shall do it again because deep down we know that the real heroes in America are those who, in their families and in their daily lives, respect the truth that we must meet the obligations and sacrifices of freedom before we claim its privileges and benefits. Deep down we know that come what may—even if it means that we must sacrifice in our personal lives—we have to stand where our Founders stood: on the belief that no one has the right to do what is wrong, that if we build self-government on a true adherence to the principles of justice, then we shall hold up a beacon of light and hope for all of humankind to understand the true destiny of mankind.

2

THE CRISIS OF CHARACTER

Freedom without restraint will inevitably become disorder.

The moral requirements of freedom are clear. According to the *Declaration of Independence*, our freedom comes from a transcendent authority—from the Creator. That means that the kind of freedom our Founding Fathers envisioned cannot be exercised without discipline. If it comes from a certain authority, it has to be exercised with some respect for that authority.

So there is a discipline inherent in the American conception of freedom. We do not have the right to do anything we please, because if we act in that way, we will be rejecting and undercutting the authority from which our freedom ultimately comes. American freedom necessarily contains within it the seeds of discipline and responsibility. These are the indispensable counterparts of our exercise of choice, and our exercise of liberty—which means that we have to have within ourselves the moral capacity to exercise that discipline.

Thus, the moral requirements of freedom are at bottom what the Founders called self-government. Self-government begins with self-control—that is to say, it begins with the ability of each of us to restrain our own passions and our own inclinations. Self-government demands at one and the same time the willingness to postpone our material gratification to the extent necessary for economic success and the discretion to limit our passions to the extent necessary to live in peace with our fellow citizens. Both of these things are prerequisites of recognizing in the individual the right to make choices for himself or herself.

The real crisis of our times is therefore, a crisis of character. It is a crisis that has been caused by our inability to admit the moral requirement of freedom. It is a crisis that has been caused by our insistence on marginalizing Truth.

This crisis of character has wrought a tremendous number of consequences—in almost every area of life. It has of course wrought dire consequences in our deteriorating family structures. But it has also wrought seriously debilitating social, political, and legal consequences.

Notice for instance, our growing obsession with rights of various kinds—covering everything from a fixation on psychosocial victimization to wholesale charges of sexual harassment in the workplace, from litigious gender equity issues to the radical gay rights agenda. All of these are directly related to this crisis of character—to the eroding moral condition of the country and of the people.

Why is that the case? To a large degree it is because we can no longer trust one another to exercise self-government.

Take, for example, the furor over sexual harassment and the myriad tangential issues that it has suddenly raised in American social life—like the codes of dating conduct and other standards for political correctness now emerging in many businesses. At one university, administration officials were actually proposing specific rules for how to move from one level of intimacy to another. Apparently, you are now supposed to stop and ask permission for each new advance across certain boundaries of intimacy. Have we really arrived at the situation where anybody who wants to go out on a date without strict legal adherence to this juridical code—or perhaps, the presence of their lawyer—is in real legal jeopardy?

This could make for some interesting dates: at each stage in the game we would all have to negotiate the terms for moving from one stage to the next; or perhaps the two parties would just sit it out while the two lawyers worked out the terms and signed the agreement.

Such a scenario is obviously absurd—and yet it is practically what we have come to these days. We still recognize it as absurd though because somewhere, deep down, we continue to believe that there ought to be certain human relationships that can be managed by individuals without the intervention of government, courts, law, the state, outside powers.

That is a natural assumption for us to make. In fact, we make that kind of assumption all the time—in all kinds of areas from the arena of family life to our interpersonal relationships. And yet, it is getting more and more dangerous to do so.

The way things are moving in the so-called children's rights movement for instance, we will not even be able to get up and hug our daughter good morning without the presence of a lawyer—or at least without taking videotapes to make sure that no unwarranted charges can be brought against us.

There is in this kind of trend, evidence not only of a kind of absurdity, evidence not only of an external push in the name of sundry group rights, but also evidence of something far deeper than that. There is evidence of a radical society-wide distrust—the sense that, at a certain level, we can't be alone with each other. I have to wonder for instance, why anyone would allow a one-on-one meeting between individuals of opposite sexes, without videotape or a witness there. These days that is a risky proposition—taking your life in your hands, or at the very least, your career.

The fact is, we can no longer maintain the expectation that people will govern themselves, that they will exercise self-control. It almost seems as if we just can't trust anyone any more.

Where has this level of radical distrust come from? To a large degree it results from a certain alteration in our concept of the human person. And that alteration can be understood if we look at another of these areas where group rights are being asserted—and that is the gay rights agenda.

Normally the terms of this discussion revolve around whether we do or do not approve of the sexual activities that a small group of individuals engage in. But let's look at it from another perspective altogether. People are now coming forward and are basically telling us that for purposes of discrimination, sexual orientation—or, more accurately, sexual behavior—must be treated like race.

Is that at all legitimate? When I got up this morning I was a black guy. When I go to bed tonight, in all probability I will still be a black guy. And no matter how much I try to talk myself out of it in the meantime, this is still going to be the case. That is because by definition this business of race is something that is really beyond my control. I know in the past people used to refer to people as being of the "colored persuasion." But that was a simply a manner of speaking—and a very inaccurate manner at that. Persuasion really has nothing to do with it whatsoever.

So, if we are going to say that sexual orientation is to be treated like race for purposes of discrimination, then we're obviously saying that sexual orientation—read, behavior—is like race, a condition beyond the individual's control.

The problem of course is that such a notion would necessarily undermine all principles of sexual responsibility and accountability—principles that are essential for certain kinds of intimate relationships, such as marriage.

When we get married we take a vow—there is an explicit understanding that we will be faithful. But if our orientation—read, behavior—is beyond our control, then when we walk out and see an attractive member of the opposite sex and we give in to temptation, who can blame us? If we should come home after the affair and our spouse detects the telltale signs and starts to call us to account we could just turn to them and you say, "Well, you, you can't raise that issue. I have an adulterous orientation. It's just something you'll have to accept."

Now, if you think that this line of reasoning is simply absurd, all you have to do is recall the recent *Time* magazine cover story that proclaimed, "Infidelity: It's In the Genes." There are indeed those who believe that we are held in the grip of indomitable animal instinct and we cannot help but do what comes naturally.

If we accept this kind of reasoning though, why we should be expected to draw the line at sexual passion? Isn't that rather unfair—discriminatory even? If we're going to have special legal protections for homosexuals, shouldn't everybody else's uncontrollable sexual orientations be protected? Shouldn't adulterers, pedophiles, rapists, and other sorts of sexual aberrants be eligible for the same benefits? Shouldn't we all be able to demand that our uncontrollable sexual behaviors be accorded the same respect and freedom from discrimination that is being demanded for gays?

And further, shouldn't that same principle of equality apply to other human passions? After all, what is it that distinguishes sexual orientation from other emotional or behavioral orientations? What if I am someone who is disposed to fly into a rage whenever anything fails to go my way? You could say I had an anger orientation, and that passion should be treated with respect. Or what if I am someone who is disposed to become uncontrollably jealous, when somebody gets something that I want? So I have a jealousy orientation. Why wouldn't that be subject to the same kind of respect? I don't understand why it is that we would want to accord one passion this kind of special legal and cultural categorization and not give it to all the passions—since it seems to me that to a certain degree they all have an equal standing in this regard: if we can't control one why is it that we can control the rest?

Of course, if we were to accept this convoluted logic we would be left with the concept of the human person which accents strict external regimentation: we are basically people out of control.

Though that may sound a bit far-fetched, in fact, I think in just about every respect our society is moving in that direction.

The modern rights movement has actually bought a concept of the human person that basically denies free will and responsibility. We are not people capable of controlling our passions and our reactions to the situations and circumstances around us. That being the case, the only way in which we can be rendered safe for one another, is for our behavior to be externally controlled and surveyed.

And we then have the problem of constructing the mechanisms for this kind of external control—ergo, restrictive regulations and controls in virtually every area of life.

What we have actually done in adopting this premise is to discard the essential assumption of self-government. This means we are now operating under a regime where genuine freedom is no longer possible. So, we have begun to substitute a regime of governmental intrusion that in the end will become little more than arbitrary rule—especially since we tend to identify the standards of law with the decisions of lawyers and the precedents of the courts.

We are trusting that kind of arbitrariness because we can no longer trust one another, and we no longer trust one another because we can no longer make assumptions about the common character of decency that we share as a people.

Thus we are facing a deep-seated moral crisis—a crisis that manifests itself partly in principle and partly in practice.

In principle it manifests itself as a rejection of the idea that there is a foundation in our lives for human justice and the observance of human justice. Most Americans once believed that there was such a foundation—but our leaders, politicians, and statesmen don't want to talk about it anymore because they claim that it involves bringing religion into politics. Indeed, there was a time when most Americans held to the notion that the only sure and secure foundation for freedom was God—the Source of unalienable rights and the Policeman stationed in every human heart. On that basis, the great American experiment in liberty originally involved the development of a moral regime that was relatively universal.

But apparently, we don't believe in that sort of thing anymore. As a result, we are attempting to reinvent America. We are trying to substitute for that basic premise all kinds of structures of legal and external control.

The problem, of course, is that it won't work. It never has. It never will. Throughout all of human history, the only thing that does work, the only thing that makes provision for freedom in human societies, is moral character. No matter how ingenious we are, no matter how creative we are, we will never find a substitute for character that is compatible with freedom.

And all we will be doing if we try, is to construct the elaborate legal rationalizations for the imposition of an ever-increasing degree of totalitarian tyranny and control. Sadly, we have already proven that—and only too well.

Indeed, the moral requirements of freedom are clear.

Two

The Hope
For the Future

At the level of common-sense conscience, the Declaration of Independence still shapes what we are as a people. Despite the betrayal and the abandonment of the elite in their pseudo-sophistication, the people themselves have no substitute for the Declaration. The elite have abandoned it without being able to articulate any substitute for it. There isn't one. And so that simple logic in the Declaration—that our rights come from God and must be respected out of respect for his authority, and therefore we have government based on consent and can require that our rights be respected—that simple logic, which from the view of ordinary people is what protects them from oppression, is what gives them the courage of their convictions when they demand that their dignity be respected. That has no substitute.

3

Revolt Against Maturity

These days maturity is just another word for old.

It is good to see that more and more people are beginning to trace the sources of America's social and economic ills to the sad disrepair of our society's moral infrastructure. Liberals are talking about welfare reform that encourages the work ethic instead of undermines it. Economic conservatives are acknowledging the role that moral discipline plays in wealth creation.

In both cases, the key insight comes from seeing people as producers, rather than passive consumers. When economic activity seduces people into seeing themselves primarily in the latter role, it's just as bad for moral fiber as rampant welfare dependency. Indeed, it may be far worse, since it affects the vast majority of our people.

The 1960s saw the beginning of a general retreat from traditional mores throughout American society, spurred by the emergence of a popular culture that emphasized materialism and hedonism. Self-fulfillment became the definition of happiness, with sexual pleasure and money (or the things money can buy) as the main barometers of its attainment. The driving force behind this culture wasn't ideological, but economic. In the decades after

World War II, mass consumption became the engine of economic expansion. The mass communications media provided the means to stimulate consumption on the scale required. But to produce the desired effect, the message conveyed by the media had to break down the moral and psychological inhibitions on consumption.

Traditional mores encouraged people to feel that self-indulgence should be limited by a sense of responsibility, obligation or moral discipline. In the context of a strong ethic of marriage and family, for example, the desire to be "sexy" was more or less confined to the youthful years before marriage and parenthood. The need for clothes or other possessions assumed to attract the opposite sex also decreased significantly once one found a dependable marriage partner. Maturity implied above all the ability to discipline and control one's desires, to reduce or eliminate personal needs that complicated or interfered with the effort to meet one's responsibilities to family and community. This was especially true for working people, whose livelihood often depended on their ability to put aside self-indulgent temptations.

The mass consumption economy made such notions seem obsolete and counterproductive. Where consumption is the law and the prophets, self-discipline is heresy. More is always better. Since maturity places limits on the desire for more, maturity is out. Adolescence comes into its own. The best consumers are perpetual teenagers, people for whom personal desires are fresh and irresistible, and who therefore find it hard to accept having any limits placed upon them. They are always wanting and needing what the market has to offer.

Of course, in the old days adolescents were mostly assumed to be dependent upon their more mature elders for the money they needed to finance their consumption. But to achieve a mass base of consumption, the link between work and maturity had to be broken. The mass consumption economy needs full-fledged earners with desires untrammeled by any limiting sense of obligation to others. It thrives on people who acquire the skills to earn, but who remain emotionally single and self-centered. It needs adults who are adolescents with a paycheck. This concept of adulthood has come to dominate the mass media, in advertising as well as entertainment. Television shows, music videos, movies and pop culture magazines glorify the successful consumer, the man or woman who "has it all." By implication, they denigrate people of limited means or self-limited desires, who lack the resources or else the ambition to be successful in this way.

These days maturity is just another word for old. It's an end point instead of a goal. So from drug addiction to AIDS to crime in the streets, we live in an era oppressed by the consequences of producing whole generations of people trapped in endless adolescence by their consuming passions.

In Shakespeare's *Coriolanus,* when Menenius invites the hero's enraged mother, Volumnia, to dinner she replies: "Anger's my meat; I sup upon myself, And so shall starve with feeding." Consuming passion means self-destruction. Not a comforting thought in the age of mass consumption economics.

4

CLEAR AND PRESENT DANGER

The administration has adopted the view that character is an irrelevant issue.

Health and Human Services Secretary Donna Shalala has sounded the alarm. Teen drug use is on the rise. According to a recent University of Michigan survey of 51,000 eighth-grade through high school students, teen smoking and drug use rose a bit last year for the first time in more than a decade.

Miss Shalala is right to be concerned, though she probably doesn't want to consider an important factor contributing to a halt in progress against teen drug abuse. Thanks especially to Nancy Reagan, among others, the 1980s became the "just say no" decade for kids. Despite ridicule from the late night comedians and other trendy barometers of the entertainment culture, Mrs. Reagan pushed an approach to drug education based on self-control.

Sadly, Donna Shalala and her cohorts in the Clinton administration represent a return to the permissiveness that conquered America's moral consciousness in the '60s. Miss Shalala herself has been a prime mover in the administration's campaign to make condoms the instrument of choice for AIDS prevention.

Given the contradictory evidence on condom effectiveness against the AIDS virus, this is a high risk approach, tantamount to playing Russian roulette with the lives and health of millions of Americans, especially among the young. But we can't expect teens to practice abstinence, can we? After all, do human beings have more sexual self-control than rabbits? The Condom Czars, Miss Shalala and the still-vocal former Surgeon General Jocelyn Elders think not. So does AIDS Czar Kristine Gebbie, who has declared herself offended by America's unwillingness to appreciate the joys of sex. So it's just say yes to sex, show self-control the door.

The same hopelessly permissive attitude prevails when the Clinton health team talks about drugs. The ever-outrageous Dr. Elders apparently thinks it's too much to expect kids to refrain from drug use. Abstinence is too hard a message there, too. So she advocates a hard look at the advantages of legalizing the drug trade. Miss Shalala's department chimes in with a chorus on the decided advantages of federal participation in needle exchange programs for drug addicts, as a way to hold down the spread of AIDS.

From the top down, the Clinton administration and its clinging cohorts offer new insight into what it means to be morally obtuse. It doesn't help that, in order to defend the president from persistent echoes of his "allegedly" very randy past, the administration has adopted the view that character is an irrelevant issue. Tell that to the thirteen-year-olds and see how they react. Actually, I think we all know how they'll react. During the teen years, passionate impulses are strong, and seem pretty irresistible. The rational human will that can in fact subordinate these impulses to higher ideas and purposes usually remains far from its full development.

In the psychological struggle between rational will and impulsive passion, genuine moral examples—what the vapid social experts of our day call "role models," as if all decent behavior is just an act—can be a fifth column on the side of responsibility infiltrating the consciousness of the young to reinforce inner inclination toward self-restraint.

Bad examples do just the opposite. What effect do you think the moral example and message we're getting from Mr. Clinton, Miss Gebbie, Dr. Elders or Miss Shalala is likely to have on a youngster teetering beside the precipice of temptation? They are creating a moral atmosphere that gives comfort to the "If it feels good, do it" mentality, offering condoms, training in sex techniques and drug legalization to foster the illusion that government can clean up the consequences of irresponsible behavior.

We live in times when just about every domestic problem we face is, at its root, a problem of moral character. Yet despite Bill Clinton's occasional manipulation of the rhetoric of "values" for political purposes, his administration steers a mistaken course between warmed-over techno-psycho-babble and barely repressed enthusiasm for moral degeneracy and self-indulgence. Given this policy direction, the resumption of a rise in drug abuse among teens is just a straw in the wind, a harsh ill wind that will whip high the already raging fires of violence, sexual promiscuity and drug addiction that are ravaging the moral infrastructure of our nation.

Donna Shalala and her permissive fellow travelers in the Clinton administration should indeed sound the alarm, but we can't expect them to be too candid in their warnings, since one clear and present danger to the moral fiber of the Republic is the one they themselves represent.

5

A Triumph
of Human Spirit

What has always especially attracted me about tennis is the primacy of moral factors.

Perhaps more than any sport except boxing, tennis epitomizes individual achievement. Victory depends on the player's physical skill and conditioning, applied intelligence, and above all what they call "mental toughness" in a situation where the singles player knows that it all comes down to him alone.

What has always especially attracted me about tennis is the primacy of moral factors. Though the best players must have superlative tennis skills, the difference between the good players and the top players isn't usually a matter of physical prowess. The person at the top doesn't always have the biggest serve, the best return of serve, the most faultless groundstrokes. The champions often win because at critical moments they can keep it all together, despite the pressures of play, the mood of the crowd, or the ups and downs of their lives off the court. They're tough competitors, who know how to be disciplined when victory is in sight, and how to keep it in mind even when things look hopeless.

Where heart is concerned, one of the greatest on the courts today is Michael Chang. During the first week of Wimbledon a few years ago, he played three five-set matches, finally losing in five sets to fellow American and friend David Wheaton. In that last match, he was down by two sets, but he kept scrambling, going after every shot, fighting off break points, using his remarkable quickness to create and exploit opportunities. Watching Mr. Chang play is like a visit to the Holy Land at Easter, thoroughly uplifting. No matter what the situation, he never loses faith, never assumes defeat or surrenders to the inevitable. It may have something do with the fact that he is himself a man of deep religious faith. Something just keeps him going.

By coincidence, the same week I watched that match I had been reading a book on *The New Politics of Poverty* by Lawrence Mead, a political science professor at New York University. He argues that the intractable problem of poverty for the so-called "underclass" isn't the result of external factors like a poor economy or racism. The main reason for this poverty is "non-work," fed by a variety of cultural and psychological factors, including a government welfare structure that doesn't include any obligation to work. Mr. Mead concludes that "Conservatives are largely correct that opportunity is available to the poor. But liberals have the more credible view of the psychology of poverty. To view the seriously poor as self-confident maximizers, as conservative analysts do, is implausible."

Mr. Mead's book is replete with interesting facts and serious analytical flaws, but his point about the misguided optimism of some conservative thinking is well-aimed. Despite all the talk about incentives, some conservatives neglect the key fact that a lack of motivation can lead people to remain passive even where opportunities exist. People who don't believe in themselves, or who surrender to hopelessness, are people who will give up without trying. They don't look for work or respond to opportunity because their spirit is broken. Unfortunately, though Mr. Mead sees the problem, and reluctantly admits that "to explain non-work, I see no avoiding some appeal to psychology or culture," the very language of his admission shows that he too misses, or refuses to discuss, the real issue. The core of motivation is moral identity. People with a strong sense of right and wrong, and a clear sentiment of their own integrity can keep striving against the odds. Such people, though, don't measure their self-worth in money terms. Yet in his chapter on "Human Nature," Mead suggests that we can't define behavior as rational "unless the goal maximized involves material gain." Then why fight on when you think you're sure to lose? Why work when you know you'll never be more than "working poor?"

Morality involves the belief that there are measures of human behavior that can't be quantified, but that must be respected. Sort of like the human spirit. Social scientists such as Mr. Mead are incompetent to deal with problems involving moral issues, since they define moral action as irrational. So, apparently, do many of the poor. Perhaps the "non-working" poor remain so because they think like social scientists, when what they really need is the spirit of Michael Chang.

6

SELF-CONTROL

Lawless ideas have lawless consequences.

A recent spate of violence in D.C. that claimed, among others, the life of a four-year-old child, attracted understandably grieved and outraged comment from first lady Hillary Clinton. She called the violence "a sick, sick symptom that we are out of control at so many levels of our society."

Observers are speculating that Mrs. Clinton's expressed interest in doing something about criminal violence on our streets and in our neighborhoods and schools signals the next item on her agenda. She will do for crime what she has done for health care. If so, we should expect to see an omnibus crime proposal that aggravates the problems we have and uses higher taxes and more centralized government control to fix things that aren't broken.

Sadly, nothing in the background or record of the Clinton administration or the Democrats in Congress offers much hope that they have even a slight inkling of the root of the crime problem. Gun control and a little more federal spending seem to be the best they can muster before their policy imagination gives out. Oh, and the need to curb the portrayal of violence in the entertainment media.

The problem is control, all right, but it's *self-control* not *gun control*. External violence is the symptom and consequence of internal lawlessness and self-indulgence.

I wonder if Mrs. Clinton understands, for instance, the intimate connection between violence on the streets and violence against unborn children in the womb? I wonder if she acknowledges the connection between casual sex and casual violence? Judging by the Clinton administration's policies on abortion and sex education, I doubt it.

President Clinton is pro-choice. He supports a position that encourages young women to believe it's better to take a human life than to take personal responsibility for the consequences of their actions. Ultimately, the pro-choice position rests on the notion that there is no law respecting life that is higher than personal convenience and gratification.

The pro-choice position is related to the "safe-sex" condom distribution approach to sex education. This approach assumes that there are certain animal passions that people, and especially young people, simply can't control: They're all going do it, so we just have to get them to do it safely. Forget the fact that the "safe sex, safer sex" slogan is a dangerous myth (Russian Roulette is arguably safer than suicide, but do we distribute pamphlets recommending it to people suffering from depression?). Forget the notion that human beings have a rational will strong enough to control our animal desires.

I would ask Mrs. Clinton why it makes sense to assume that the capacity for self-control we neglect when dealing with sexual passions will suddenly reappear when dealing with anger, jealousy, fear, greed, pride, and other passions that, if unrestrained, lead to violence. Each passion is somewhat different, but the faculty that restrains passion can be the same in every case.

People who can't talk themselves out of irresponsible sex, even when it leads to life-destroying violence, won't be too persuasive when it comes to other irresponsible acts, even when they lead to life-destroying violence. The young woman says, "I must kill this innocent unborn child to save my womanhood." The young gangster says, "I must kill an innocent stranger so I can prove my manhood." Mrs. Clinton says the first is a right and the second an outrage. Yet both exhibit the same ruthlessly self-regarding passion.

Crime and violence aren't just social facts, or empirical phenomena. They are moral realities. Moral problems can't be addressed with external solutions such as gun control or condom distribution. They need internal remedies. Though we shy away from the subject these days, most decent people know in their hearts that the only solution to these moral problems is moral education. The basic principle of all moral education is respect for our moral faculty, i.e., the human capacity to act rationally, to discipline passion in order to prevent immoral consequences. Mrs. Clinton claims to be concerned about crime, yet the Clinton administration supports positions on the most critical moral issues that deny and undermine the moral faculty.

Mrs. Clinton, lawless ideas have lawless consequences.

7

RELIGION AND POLITICS

The Founders believed that the idea of freedom could not survive without an appeal to God.

According to press reports, Bill Clinton is a big fan of Stephen Carter's influential book, *The Culture of Disbelief*. Until the effort was derailed by published allegations of persistent adultery during his last days as governor of Arkansas, Mr. Clinton was engaged in a major effort to demonstrate his respect for religious faith.

What better way for him to symbolize this respect than to express admiration for Mr. Carter's book, which purports to be an expose of the ways in which American law and politics trivialize religious devotion. Unfortunately, Mr. Carter's work only gives the appearance of taking religion seriously, without in fact doing so. Maybe that's why the present occupant of the White House finds it so appealing.

Mr. Carter asserts that "what was wrong with the 1992 Republican Convention was not the effort to link the name of God to secular political ends. What was wrong was the choice of secular ends to which the name of God was linked." We would be partially mistaken if statements like this lead us to conclude that the whole intention of Mr. Carter's book is to make it possible for liberals such as Mr. Clinton to overcome their embarrassed hostility toward religion long enough to manipulate religious feeling for their political ends.

Since he is a black American, Mr. Carter may be motivated by the fact that the Civil Rights movement, which overthrew legally sanctioned racial discrimination in America was thoroughly saturated by religious rhetoric and convictions. As he notes at several points in the book, when people impugn the propriety of religious motives in our political life "equal calumny is implicitly heaped upon the mass protest wing of the civil rights movement, which was openly and unashamedly religious in its appeals as it worked to impose its moral vision on, for example, those who would rather segregate their restaurants."

This view of the civil rights movement perfectly illustrates the vitiating flaw in Mr. Carter's approach to the issue of religion in American life. The Reverend Martin Luther King Jr. didn't believe he was imposing his moral vision on the practitioners of segregation. He believed that he spoke to and for the moral principles on which the nation is based. When he used the fervent religious rhetoric of his Christian faith to articulate those principles, he did them no violence because they were themselves articulated using a less fervent version of the same religious rhetoric. Like Abraham Lincoln before him, Dr. King relied on the words and influence of the *Declaration of Independence*, and on its hold upon the conscience of the American people.

The *Declaration* explicitly embodies an argument that relies upon religious belief. Using this argument, it states the first principles of the American nation, the common beliefs that define our identity as a people. The American Founders believed that a regime based on the idea of human equality in freedom could not survive without an appeal to God, as the source of human rights. This conviction led Thomas Jefferson to ask "can the liberties of a nation be thought secure when we have removed their only firm basis, a conviction in the minds of the people that these liberties are the gift of God? That they are not to be violated but with His wrath?"

It may be possible to make out an affirmative answer to Jefferson's query. Nothing in the contemporary condition of American society, however, suggests this is so. In any case, both the *Declaration* and the prudential judgment behind it ascribe to religious belief a fundamental role in the assertion and maintenance of political liberty. More than this, they suggest that a particular religious belief—specifically, monotheism—may be indispensable. Though Mr. Carter purports to take religion seriously, he never deals with its claim to be the *sine qua non* that secures the characteristic common good of the American polity.

Yet neglect of this claim is the most critical way in which the liberal approach to law and politics trivializes religious belief. Religious believers should therefore be wary of the praise heaped on Mr. Carter's work by liberals such as Bill Clinton. They remain unwilling to give religious faith its due.

8

A MORAL LEGACY

A moral legacy, not race or skin color, is the foundation of the black American identity.

When an eminent black American scholar with more than sixty years of experience pronounces the key tenets of Afrocentrism to be little more than modern myth-making, when he speaks in strong defense of the wisdom to be garnered from the study of classic texts from ancient Greece and Rome, will his salvo cause academics manning the ramparts of political correctness to dive for cover? Probably not.

In a recent commencement address at the University of Maryland, former Howard University professor Frank Snowden simply spoke the truth, as years of study and research have given him to see it. That's what a scholar is supposed to do, regardless of politics. This means of course that Mr. Snowden also rejects the key tenet of political correctness, which subordinates the search for truth to the desire for political justice. Unfortunately, as Mr. Snowden pointed out in his address, this can lead to a situation where the passion for justice relies on distortions and falsehoods.

What we call Afrocentrism today emerged originally in response to the lies and distortions long employed by racists to denigrate blacks and justify treating us as inferior. In Booker T. Washington's day—around the time Frank Snowden was born— a score of books appeared aimed at countering these distortions. C. T. Walker's *Appeal to Caesar* (1900) was among the first to refer to Egyptian civilization as evidence of past black achievements. In *The Ammonian or Hametic Origin of the Ancient Greeks, Cretans and all the Celtic Races* (1905), Joseph E. Hayne purported to show that blacks created Greek and Cretan civilizations, and that the British empire owed its greatness to the Negro ancestry of the Celts. A pamphlet by W. L. Hunter, first published in 1901, aimed to prove that *Jesus Christ had Negro Blood in His Veins*. Some such works were more rhetoric than history, but others, such as W. E. B. Dubois's *The Negro* (1915) offered scholarly arguments that gave Americans who rated enough to read them their first serious look at the African heritage of American blacks.

In his important work *Negro Thought in America, 1880–1915,* August Meier rightly notes "the compensatory and psychological role the Negro history movement played, for it gave dignity in the face of insults and provided arguments for equality in the face of assertions of inferiority."

So Afrocentrism wasn't born yesterday. Unfortunately, it still bears the marks of its reactionary origins. Works produced in reaction against demeaning racial stereotypes begin by accepting race or skin color as their analytical category. The author then searches through history looking for examples that fall within this category.

Whatever the results, the work remains within the confines of the original racial category. Like someone struggling in quick-sand, the researcher's efforts to struggle against racism simply involve him more deeply in its worldview. Indeed, as Mr. Snowden points out in his address, the researcher ends up seeing racial categories even where none existed, thus allowing racism to triumph intellectually over history itself.

Does the existence of this pitfall mean black Americans should simply reject the purveyors of ethnicity? Does it mean surrendering to the view that black Americans have no distinctive ethnic identity? If race is not the defining principle of that identity, what common bond do they have, beyond their common heritage of enslavement, discrimination, and oppression?

But what other heritage is needed? Too many black Americans look to Africa to find a basis for their identity because they cannot find it in themselves to claim their true heritage with pride. They are ashamed of their slave ancestry, ashamed of all those who lead rebellions or guided fugitives through the underground railroad, all the ordinary folk who simply lived as best they could under the yoke. They apparently haven't yet realized that the survival of black people in America, through slavery, racist assaults, and economic deprivation, is one of the greatest sagas of the human spirit the world has ever seen.

When will we stop looking for glorious empires along the Niger or the Nile, and begin to truly appreciate the more lasting monument of values, endurance, and faith that black Americans built along the Potomac and the Mississippi? That moral legacy, not race or skin color or any other material thing, is the strong foundation of the black American identity. Isn't it time we began to reclaim and build upon it?

9

OUTING THE LEFT

Why are petty, close-minded bigots allowed to call themselves liberals?

Besides provoking a flurry of interest in black conservatives, the presence of Clarence Thomas on the Supreme Court has apparently aroused the nastier instincts of some of his supposedly liberal critics.

Take, for example, the outburst by black columnist and TV commentator Carl Rowan: "If they had put David Duke on, I wouldn't scream as much because they would look at David Duke for what he is. If you gave Clarence Thomas a little flour on his face, you'd think you had David Duke talking."

Apparently, if we put a little flour on his face, Judge Thomas might have some hope of getting a fair hearing from political bigots. Since he's black, fairness need not apply.

Mr. Rowan has always been a champion practitioner of the vicious racial intimidation through which some black leaders have tried to keep the black community in the grip of political and intellectual totalitarianism. Disagree with them and you're instantly excommunicated from the black race, accused of being a "white-thinking black," an "Oreo cookie" or, at the very least, a foot-shuffling "Uncle Tom."

Mr. Rowan's knee-jerk bigotry comes as no surprise to me. In 1988, when the Maryland Republican Party nominated me for the U.S. Senate, he wrote a column dismissing my candidacy as a "token" because I was black. He didn't interview me. He didn't look at my background or experience in government. He looked only at my skin color and boldly prejudged the situation.

As it turned out, nearly 40 percent of Maryland's voters disagreed with him, a showing that equaled or exceeded that of the Republican candidates in the two preceding Senate races.

This is, of course, precisely the kind of prejudice the great champions of the civil rights struggle fought against. Yet people like Mr. Rowan routinely practice it, while lambasting others for betraying the civil rights cause.

Why are petty, close-minded bigots allowed to call themselves "liberals"? Until it was hijacked by these covert totalitarians, the word liberal implied a generous, fair-minded approach to issues. It implied a willingness to give all sides a hearing. Now it refers to intellectual fascists who deem themselves the good guys and say their way is the only way.

Another clear example of this bigotry has emerged in "know-nothing" anti-Catholic slurs and innuendo against Judge Thomas by advocates of abortion. Though the political archetype of contemporary liberal idealism, John Kennedy, was himself a practicing Catholic, these virulent, single-issue ideologues feel justified in stirring up the corrosive venom of religious bigotry in their zeal to take Judge Thomas apart. Yet the Catholics who now sit on the court were confirmed without such scurrilous attacks.

Since Judge Thomas is black, the pro-abortion zealots think it's safe to show their religious bigotry in ways they wouldn't dream of doing if he were white.

Contemporary liberals always have suffered from an undercurrent of condescending bigotry. That's why the liberal stereotypes of the "victims" of society correspond so closely to the old racist stereotypes that victimized blacks in the first place.

Today, when they say "helpless," do they still mean "lazy"? Today, when they say "disadvantaged," do they still mean "inferior"? Today, when they say "underclass," don't they still mean second-class citizens?

As victims, blacks still are placed conveniently to be looked down upon. If a black person dares to look them in the eye, to think for himself, to claim with pride a role in his own achievements, they rush to stomp him down, just as racist mobs in the old South took it upon themselves to deal peremptorily with what they called "uppity" blacks.

Clarence Thomas is such a person and the lynch mob is forming. Some blacks such as Carl Rowan are helping to knot the rope. Others such as Benjamin Hooks are hesitating, sensing, I think, the trap laid out before them. Somewhere in their hearts they know that even though the ideologues say they're "Borking" a conservative, in reality they're just lynching another black.

10

THE RACE CARD AND LIBERALISM

Domination by the state has undermined black America's traditional reliance on family and church.

The cover of a recent issue of *Emerge* magazine—which styles itself *Black America's Newsmagazine*—offers a doctored photo of Supreme Court Justice Clarence Thomas wearing a sly look, with a handkerchief tied around his head.

The cover story bears the headline "Betrayed: Clarence Thomas' Former Supporters." Both the cover photo and the article smack of the diseased mentality of the liberal black establishment in America today. Name calling and ridicule take the place of common sense and reason in the establishment's attacks on black Americans who don't subscribe to the party line. The gist of the article is simple. Some liberal blacks supported Justice Thomas' elevation to the Supreme Court because they thought he would alter his conservative views once confirmed. He hasn't. His votes on the court have been entirely consistent with his known and expressed views prior to his confirmation. Therefore, he duped them, and they feel betrayed.

In America, during the Clinton reign of lies, the sight of a public figure who is exactly what he appears to be may seem like cause for chagrin, particularly to the establishment blacks who supported Mr. Clinton so enthusiastically during the election.

Black liberals still suffer from the bigoted belief that anyone who disagrees with them must be pretending. This despite the fact that their approach to the problems of black America has not only failed, but has produced enormous tragedy in the black community. They march in gay pride parades, preach condom distribution, destroy black pride with their continual litany of black hopelessness and failure.

Abandoning the black community's traditional emphasis on family, religious faith, and self-reliance, they assiduously pursue a strategy of dependence on government spending and government power. Their materialistic liberalism shoulders aside the black American value system that gives primacy to morality and spirituality. Large-scale reliance on the welfare system obscures the community's traditional belief in hard work, self-reliance and self-improvement as the keys to survival and progress.

Most importantly, domination by the impersonal structures of the bureaucratic state has undermined or pushed aside black America's traditional reliance on family and church as the roots of personality and security.

When they surrendered to big government paternalism, the black liberal leadership abandoned the foundations of black America's moral identity, which were in fact the foundations of our survival as individuals and as a people.

The results have been devastating. Though the black family structure survived all the assaults of racism and economic repression, it has virtually collapsed under the crushing weight of the welfare mentality spawned by liberal paternalism. The black work ethic survived the degenerative influence of decades of wickedly creative discouragements to economic initiative and enterprise. Yet it has been dangerously weakened by the liberal ideology of victimization, which makes racism an all too easy excuse for spiritual sloth and physical self-destruction.

The liberal black establishment hates Justice Thomas because he openly departs from their failed ideology. He and other black conservatives—including, I suppose, myself—are like the little boy in the old fairy tale. Through our unwillingness to silently accept their irrational dogma, we pose the risk of revealing that this emperor has no clothes, and, what is more, leaving the black community naked to its enemies.

The black liberal leaders attend summits with gang chieftains. They dance with glee when riotous thugs escape the consequences of their acts. They fight to have the justice system deal more leniently with the criminals who prey upon the streets and neighborhoods where decent black folks struggle to survive. Instead of self-control, they preach condom distribution, pushing black youth in particular into a deadly game of sexual Russian Roulette.

All the while the people who have always been the true heart and soul of the black community are ignored—the kids who hit the books instead of the streets, the people who fill the churches instead of the jails, the men who go to the altar instead of the nightclubs, facing up to the difficulties of marriage and real fatherhood even though it means burdensome work and responsibility. No summits are called that speak to their interests. Indeed, on issues from abortion to school choice, from gay rights to excessive taxation, their feelings are trampled upon and their values betrayed. But that's a cover story you won't read in *Emerge*.

11

WELFARISM
AND ETHNIC ENMITY

A sense of helplessness breeds enormous frustration.

The tragic and violent clashes between blacks and Jews in places such as the Crown Heights neighborhood in Brooklyn are unhappily not the product of a unique and isolated set of circumstances.

As I have traveled the country during the past two years, I have heard more and more about the rising tensions, misunderstandings, and angry passions afflicting black and Jewish relations in urban neighborhoods, on college campuses, and in the workplace.

It's hard for me to understand why these two groups should be at odds. Both are minorities, have experienced harsh discrimination, and because of that experience, share a deep commitment to equal justice, civil rights and social progress.

Through the prolonged holocaust of the slave trade, blacks plumbed the depths of greedy inhumanity. In the Nazi extermination camps, Jews felt the awful weight of unbridled human evil. This terrible parallel should contain the seeds of an unbreakable bond between the two peoples, for we have both looked the devil in the eye, yet never given him our souls.

But it doesn't seem to work that way any more. Jews have been oppressed, but today the Jewish community is, on the whole, one of America's most impressive stories of material success. Meanwhile, nearly half the black community continues to be mired in poverty and crime, its social fabric disintegrating. Mobs of young blacks roam the streets in Crown Heights and appear to resent and hate Jews, who have become for them a symbol of the success and influence they have not achieved.

Yet Jewish community leaders, intellectuals and political activists have always been in the forefront of the liberal movements that sought greater government action to deal with the economic and social problems of poor blacks. Jewish voters have supported the liberal advocates of these programs, and seconded their arguments that more of our society's resources should be devoted to state-sponsored action to help the poor. Given that record, many people in the Jewish community are bewildered, and themselves increasingly resentful and angry about the unwarranted expressions of anti-Semitism coming from black communities and seconded or tolerated by many black leaders.

I believe that, unwittingly, Jewish supporters of the government–dominated welfare state approach to the economic and social problems of the black community helped to create the mentality that now produces anger and anti-Semitism in black neighborhoods. Welfare state socialism encourages a sense of powerlessness and helplessness in its clients and their communities. This sense of helplessness breeds enormous frustration and makes people susceptible to demagogic appeals that offer scapegoats instead of workable solutions.

"Since I can't get up, I'll bring you down." It's not an answer, but at least it's something to do.

Welfare state socialism also inhibits the social integration of the black community across class lines, in ways that would impel successful blacks to build the structures that reach back into the community in order to draw others along with them.

Middle-class blacks have acted as if political support for government action and programs is an effective substitute for their own organizational efforts. That's why the agendas of groups such as the NAACP and the Black Caucus have become increasingly irrelevant to the real challenges faced in black communities. There is a vacuum where the black community needs an active, effective middle-class network dedicated to community action.

Jewish people can do something to help remedy this void. Well-intentioned Jewish people, as well as middle-class blacks who really care about the community's future, could reconsider their allegiance to welfare state socialism. If it works so well, why didn't the Jewish community rely upon it? Instead, Jews developed one of the most effective self-help networks in the world. The key to its success is the ability to mobilize the successful people in the Jewish community in support of efforts to aid the rest. Blacks need to do the same.

The critical mass of successful and well-to-do blacks exists today. Jewish leaders and activists understand the technology for mobilizing such community elites better than anyone. Both communities need to concentrate on developing cooperative programs to allow blacks to share in and master that technology.

Then the successful black middle class can begin to deal with underclass resentment in the right way, by developing the internal structures of self-help that will address its causes.

12

BLACKS AND THE GOP

Republicans and conservatives should make a major effort to break with the past.

We may never know the whole truth behind the flap caused by reported efforts of certain Republican Party operatives to bribe black clergymen in New Jersey—efforts designed to discourage blacks from voting. At first the chief strategist for the party, Ed Rollins, quipped that they had indeed made the payments. Later he denied it.

So, did the Republicans actually cross the line in their efforts to suppress black voter turnout on Election Day? Did any of New Jersey's black clergy agree to aid and abet the self-disenfranchisement of the state's black voters?

Whatever answers emerge over time, the whole flap should impress on everyone the ugly consequences of the present almost institutionalized enmity between the black community and the Republican Party. It hurts Republicans, it hurts black Americans, and it damages the political system as a whole.

The Republican campaign may not have gone to the illegitimate extremes Ed Rollins claimed in their efforts to "lighten the turnout" in the black community. Anyone familiar with Republican politics knows, though, that reducing black voter turnout is a standard goal, and hoped-for outcome, of Republican strategists. This complicates life enormously for black Republicans, since it means folks in the GOP leadership will work at cross-purposes with any efforts to carry the Republican message into heavily black precincts. They will even undercut a potentially successful black Republican candidacy out of fear that increased black interest in the election will work to the detriment of other Republicans on Election Day. This may explain why the only black Republicans in Congress today come from districts where black voters aren't a critical factor.

This self-defeating approach results from the myopic unwillingness of some GOP leaders and political consultants to abandon defensive tactics against the black community, and go on the offensive in search of black support. This myopia persists despite every indication that black voters share many of the GOP's conservative values and issue positions. A third to half of blacks in polling samples routinely identify themselves as conservative. On issues such as crime and welfare reform, majorities of voting blacks have supported views in line with GOP positions. Even on an issue such as abortion, roughly half of the black electorate voices opposition to unlimited abortion rights, though black Americans are a special target of the pro-abortion propagandists.

These facts don't translate into electoral support at least in part because the GOP doesn't actively pursue black support. To be sure, at meetings and conferences black conservatives are put on display in support of Republican issue positions. But interest in black conservatives isn't a two-way street. In the real world, what counts most is the mobilization of organizational and financial networks in support of the efforts black Americans are making to address problems that particularly burden the black community—such as the disintegration of family life—in ways that reflect conservative values and principles. Many black churches, for instance, are making heroic efforts to re-establish the traditional strength of the black family, to rebuild the strong ethic of work and sacrifice that was characteristic in the black American community before the pernicious effects of the bureaucratic welfare state. Republicans should be seeking out and supporting the black ministers and congregations who are mounting these efforts, instead of fantasizing about bribing the clergy to suppress black voter participation.

Republicans and conservatives should make a major effort to break with past defensive attitudes and behavior. One step might be the establishment of an activist, grassroots-oriented institute to identify and give financial support to ongoing efforts by black Americans that represent workable alternatives to the debilitating, family-killing, spirit destroying dependency fostered by the liberal welfare state. The key here is to work with the black churches—not as political pawns to be manipulated as the Democrats do—at election time with bribes and government patronage, but as the independent institutions through which black Americans have traditionally worked for the betterment of their community.

The other day I happened to say something about the black community to a friendly acquaintance at one of the conservative-leaning think tanks in Washington. He began his response by noting in an offhand way that "well, there's really no such thing as the black community is there?" He meant, I think, that not all black Americans think alike—a very good point—but he also meant that, apart from negative things like discrimination and poverty, black Americans have nothing in common—an untrue and, therefore, a very bad point.

Conservatives and Republicans need to overcome their unwillingness to see the black community—as distinct from a few black individuals—in a positive light, in order to start working with the black community's institutions toward positive goals. The Rollins flap could produce something more beneficial than fodder for the media talk shows if it helps to open more eyes to this necessity.

13

A Triumph of Literacy

Blacks managed to continue their educational progress despite declining government support.

Back in the nineteenth century, prior to the end of slavery, most Southern states, by law or custom, strongly discouraged education for black people. The then-dominant slave culture generally reflected the view that learning contributed to rebelliousness among the enslaved.

After the Civil War, however, it quickly became evident that among formerly enslaved blacks there was a passionate thirst for education. In hundreds of schools throughout what had been the Confederacy, blacks of all ages sought the knowledge they had been denied, leading to what Booker T. Washington referred to as the spectacle of "a whole race trying to go to school."

During the immediate post–Civil War years, this aspiration found support from both public and private sources. The enormous challenge of educating a group that was 95 percent illiterate meant, however, that by 1880 the illiteracy rate among black Americans was still a very high 70 percent. In the meantime, Reconstruction ended, and in the South (where more than 90 percent of all black Americans lived) a regime of political, economic, and social repression was rapidly replacing any efforts to aid the advancement of the formerly enslaved people. There was no federal funding, and Southern states refused to spend anything close to adequate amounts on education for blacks.

In his work *Black Self-Determination*, the historian V. P. Franklin summarizes the remarkable period that followed. Between 1880 and 1910, "despite decreasing public expenditures for black public education, the masses of Afro-Americans had become literate. Du Bois, U.S. Census Officials, and others accepted as basically accurate the statistical fact that the 70 percent illiteracy rate—defined as inability to write—among Afro-Americans had dropped to about 30 percent in 1910."

During a visit I paid to Seattle, a friend of mine—who happens to be black and conservative—told me about a debate she had with a woman—who happened to be black and liberal—who argued that black Americans have never made any progress in their history without a government initiative. Where have I heard that before? This assertion is repeated like a religious mantra by the liberals who act as budget shills for the public sector bureaucracies. Yet it bespeaks such a willful ignorance of black history that I sometimes suspect a conscious intention to demean black people, and belittle what we achieved for ourselves in the day when every hand, including especially that of the government, was against us.

When he seeks to explain how blacks managed to continue their educational progress despite declining government support, Mr. Franklin says "we must look to the cultural context of literacy for Afro-America." This means the black church and the black family. "Afro-Americans in the United States were among those Protestants who believed that the way to achieve salvation and personal deliverance was to know the Word of God, and live it.

"Thus many Afro-Americans learned to read and write in various religious settings, such as Sunday School classes and Sabbath Schools, within their own communities. Afro-American families not only preserved and passed on cultural values supporting education and social advancement, but also taught their children to read and write as part of the parental responsibility for the 'Christian education' of the younger generation." As with so much else in the history of black Americans, it was a matter of faith, practically applied.

When will public policy that affects the black community begin to reflect the real facts of black history? When will we stop accepting approaches to social challenges such as poverty or education based on the false assumptions of black incapacity and helplessness that the sycophants of bureaucratic power use to justify its grab for more resources? When will we begin to demand policies that reflect the strengths, the character, and the positive values that are the real heritage of black America?

14

Making Welfare Safe for Families

Welfare and welfare reform both assume that the family unit is broken and can't be fixed.

Given President Clinton's cynical disregard for most of his major campaign positions, no one will be surprised if his expressed interest in reforming the welfare system evaporates in the face of expected opposition from the usual ultra-liberal opponents of welfare reform.

However, on this issue he has a very good chance to forge a coalition of Republicans and sensible Democrats who know that most taxpayers, whatever their backgrounds, are sick to death of a costly system that encourages and perpetuates poverty. Both the House Republicans and the Clinton administration support an approach that would limit welfare without work to two years while expanding help for the working poor, including opportunities to develop savings. The aim is to finally correct the perverse incentive structure of the existing system, which seems to enforce idleness and penalize people who work hard and try to save a little of what they earn.

It has taken too long to get some people, particularly on the Democratic side, to accept the fact that common-sense reforms are urgently needed. It's not clear even now that the Democratic leadership in Congress will give welfare reform top priority, despite the lip service being paid to the need for budgetary restraint.

So it may not be a good time to point out that current proposals for reform don't go far enough. They entirely neglect the damaging impact that the rules and administration of the system have had on family structure. The system discourages marriage. It promotes single-parent, female-headed households. Much evidence indicates that, like a person standing on one leg, such households are inherently more unstable, economically and socially, than two-parent homes. That's at least one reason we all have such admiration for the strength and courage of working poor mothers who manage to sustain a wholesome family environment against the odds.

Current proposals could exacerbate this discrimination against the traditional family structure. They will force poor mothers out of the home and into the work force, despite evidence that children benefit from a stay-at-home parent, especially in the early years. They will do nothing to encourage a responsible male presence in poor families, despite much evidence that the absence of decent male role models contributes greatly to violent and self-destructive behavior, especially among teen-age males.

The core of the welfare system is a program called Aid to Families with Dependent Children. In fact, it should be called Aid to—Mostly Female—Individuals with Dependent Children. Yet unless we do something to make welfare safe for two-parent families, we will end up once again doing more harm than good. Though it's not politically correct to say so, we need a welfare system that encourages men and women to get married and stay married. It's ominously ironic that the only hint of this in current proposals is an effort to improve collection of child support payments. This approach assumes that the family unit is broken and can't be fixed.

After decades of discriminating against the marriage partnership, we need a welfare system that discriminates in its favor. Instead of paying what amounts to a baby bonus to unwed mothers, we should find ways to provide a marriage bonus to men and women who are willing to take on the tough but vital responsibilities of married life.

Unfortunately, present proposals merely add a work requirement to the baby bonus policy, and that's not good enough. Poor children need stable homes and intimate role models for the development of their characters and human relationships, particularly relations between the sexes. They won't get this from reforms that at best will result in more working mothers and a greater demand for state-controlled day care.

It's right and necessary to encourage work rather than idleness. But for real welfare reform, we need to do more than fix the economic illogic of the welfare system, we need to work at mending the family structure it has helped to undermine.

15

THE RIGHTS RAGE

Both sides in the debate over homosexuality need to back off a bit.

Can we add "sexual orientation" to the list of protected categories under our civil rights laws without violating the constitutional guarantee against government interference with freedom of religion?

Anxiety about the answer to that question may be one of the things fueling moves around the country against pro-gay civil rights legislation. Particularly in the Bible-believing Christian community, people fear that such legislation will be used to force Christian churches to accept homosexual participation in church or church-sponsored activities, or to prosecute for hate crimes those who preach from the Bible's clear condemnation of homosexual acts (Leviticus 18:22, 20:13).

Religious freedom is a First Amendment right. In several cases, the settlers who established the Colonies that eventually became the first states came to the New World to escape religious persecution. They wanted the right to live their lives according to their religious beliefs. Since these days many people regard religion as a peripheral part of life, it's not easy for them to understand just what that means. For true believers, religion permeates every aspect of their lives—what they do, what they feel, what they respect, what they condemn. In India, for instance, someone who murders a cow in a Hindu neighborhood will doubtless be killed in the ensuing riot. The same would be true of someone who throws lard into a Mosque. Such acts are, in the biblical phrase, abominations (literally, bad omens) for Hindus and Muslims. They give rise to the deepest feelings of revulsion and aversion because devout Hindus or Muslims believe they invite divine wrath. They are, therefore, bad omens, harbingers of terrible punishments to come.

If the practice of religion means anything, it has to include the right to avoid and condemn those things considered hateful to the moral precepts of the religion. Historically, it has also included the right to raise one's children to respect the same precepts. If the government acts to prevent such practices, or to establish contrary precepts, isn't this interference with the free exercise of religion? Isn't it in fact the establishment of a contrary religious code?

Homosexuals today are not just insisting that other people leave them alone. They are insisting that others respect them. Yet as many Christians read the Bible, the biblical God declares unequivocally, "Thou shalt not lie with mankind as with womankind; It is abomination." According to their religion, homosexuality cannot be respected; it must be condemned.

We will probably deal more effectively with the whole issue of homosexual rights when we realize that it is inescapably bound up with the issue of religious freedom and the meaning of religious tolerance. People who practice homosexuality reject the biblical doctrine that condemns it. They feel differently about that religious precept, just as some people feel differently than Muslims about pork or Hindus about sacred cows.

Under our secular doctrine of religious freedom, the government has no right to tell these homosexuals they must believe the Bible or practice the biblical moral code. That's why laws against their sexual practices should be repealed, unless some purely secular justification can be advanced to support them—our laws against murder for instance, are consonant with biblical teaching, but that's not why we have such laws.

On the other hand, the government also has no right to tell Bible-believing Christians that they must violate their religious conscience by respecting what the Bible condemns, or allowing their children to be educated in doctrines that contradict their biblical beliefs. If we use state power to enforce the view that homosexuality cannot be condemned, or public money to finance educational programs aimed at encouraging respect for homosexuality, we will be doing just that.

In a sense this means that both sides in the debate over homosexuality need to back off a bit. Homosexuals should realize that the more they push for legal enforcement of their "right" to exist, the more explicitly state action will shock and disturb other religious beliefs and practices. Already the veil of civil rights rhetoric is being ripped away to reveal what is essentially a religious controversy. In such a controversy, the government under our Constitution has no right to take sides unless some clear, secular public interest is affected.

Given the threat from AIDS, and the increasingly clear recognition that the breakdown of the traditional family is contributing to crime, drug abuse, poor educational performance, etc., my guess is that, on public interest grounds, the anti-gays will have the best of it.

The pendulum of permissiveness reached its high point the day Bill Clinton was elected. Before it swings too far the other way, it might be wise for gay rights activists to quit while they're ahead.

16

EDUCATION
AND LIBERAL SHIBBOLETHS

Should the lives and futures of young people be sacrificed to ideological agendas?

People in Detroit recently learned firsthand what happens when a community's common-sense efforts to respond to the critical needs of its children come up against one of the key shibboleths of the radical liberal creed.

The Detroit school system wanted to try the idea of all-male academies, with a curriculum that stresses discipline, civic responsibility and high academic standards, and that places a special emphasis on African and African-American history. The schools would be open to all races, but aimed especially at young black males.

U.S. District Judge George Woods decided that this would discriminate against the city's young females and struck down the idea. "There is no evidence," he said, "the school system is failing males because girls attend schools with them."

Of course, the idea wasn't meant to discriminate against the city's female population, but rather to deal with what everyone acknowledges to be a deep life-and-death crisis for its young black males.

Instead of being blinded by knee-jerk ideological assumptions, Judge Woods should have shown some respect for the judgment of the people who live with the crisis daily. Their common sense may be a more reliable guide than the pseudo-scientific manipulation of statistics that often passes for evidence these days among so-called social scientists.

Community support for the all-male academy idea was strong precisely because local people understand that in many neighborhoods today, inner-city black males both face and help to create an extraordinarily dangerous environment.

They need special help and attention. Is it better to give it to them in all-male schools or in the all-male prisons they now populate in disproportionate numbers?

For years, the welfare system has given special help to black females while neglecting and humiliating black males.

Young blacks from single-parent female-headed households are often deprived of effective and responsible male role models, and have no experience of healthy male bonding. They end up getting their sense of authority and personality from the criminal element that dominates the streets.

To prove their masculinity, they rely upon violence, and upon the physical and sexual abuse of the young women in their community. Films such as *New Jack City* and *Boyz N the Hood* have shocked general audiences around the country, but they depict a brutal reality that is literally eating some communities alive.

The traditional coeducational public school model has not worked to address this problem. Apparently it offers very little to remedy the negative construction of the male ego fostered by the inner-city welfare state.

Coeducation also abets the premature heightening of sexual interest and activity that unfortunately distracts and preoccupies the young in so many inner-city communities. Properly developed and socialized, human sexuality is a great blessing. Prematurely unleashed in communities with greatly weakened family structures, it has proven to be deadly.

Obviously, all-male academies are not appropriate everywhere. In communities with strong family structures, sexual socialization takes place through healthy interaction between parents and children. Where the family structure has been weakened or destroyed, however, different approaches may be needed.

Should the lives and futures of young black men, desperately in need of these approaches, be sacrificed to ideological agendas that reflect the elitist concerns of comfortable, upper middle class white liberals? These same people supported the creation of the welfare state that helped destroy the social infrastructure of the black community. Now they want to quash community-based efforts to correct their disastrous handiwork.

This is wrong, stupid, and unfair. In Detroit and elsewhere around this country, the dogmatic liberal judges and ideologues should get out of the way and let communities seek answers to their problems. Let the people go. God knows they can't make matters much worse than the so-called experts have, and their common sense may be our best shot at making things better.

17

ACCENT ON THE NEGATIVES?

A community should be ashamed of its criminal element.

At 7:00 P.M. on Tuesday, September 14, 1991, Warren McCleskey died in Georgia's electric chair. The execution brought to an end a long saga that began with the slaying in 1978 of Atlanta Police Officer Frank Schlatt during a robbery.

For several years some top civil rights organizations, including the Southern Christian Leadership Conference made McCleskey's case a *cause célèbre*. At one point Nelson Mandela was induced to make a plea on his behalf.

Warren McCleskey was black—as are a disproportionate number of the prisoners on death row around the country, as are a disproportionate number of the inmates in America's prisons. Citing those facts, some people want us to believe that the fortunes and misfortunes of America's criminal element are somehow especially a black problem, deserving a disproportionate amount of attention from organizations committed to addressing the problems of the black community.

I wonder, though, whether that conclusion doesn't mislead us into letting the problem dictate our actions instead of the solution. As a parent, I know that one always has to be careful not to give attention to one's children in proportion to their misbehavior. That teaches the wrong kind of lesson, leading well-behaved kids to conclude that misbehavior merits more parental interest. If a community pays an inordinate amount of attention to the troublemakers and miscreants, while leaving the decent folks to look out for themselves, don't we run the risk of encouraging the bad guys and leaving the struggling decent people without hope?

We can't be indifferent if our justice system grossly miscarries, trampling the rights of an individual. But in McCleskey's case, for example, the supposed injustice lay in the fact that the prosecutors made deals with some of McCleskey's pals in exchange for their help in getting him to admit the crime.

Now, our police and prosecutors will surely be in a bad way if we decide never to accept the evidence one criminal offers against another. After the fact, McCleskey claimed that, though he participated in the armed robbery, he wasn't the one who actually gunned down Officer Schlatt. Still, his fate may serve as a warning to would-be armed robbers that a little bad luck may blur the fatal line that separates a few years in prison from the crushing voltage of an electric chair. To avoid that risk, avoid the robbery, since you can't be sure what people will believe once the bullets stop flying and someone is dead.

I can't say that I think it would be a bad thing if would-be criminals believed that bad luck could send them to the chair even when bad intentions don't. I'm not sure it's a good thing if they believe that respected organizations will spring to their defense whenever a little doubt intervenes between them and their just deserts. Crime should be a risky business, one that easily leads to harsh consequences when things go even a bit wrong.

I also think a community should be ashamed of its criminal element, not seek statistical excuses to turn them into special social causes.

For decades black Americans suffered through all kinds of oppression and discrimination. Yet for the most part, black people didn't succumb to crime and other forms of depravity. We despised criminals. The blacks who turn to crime today, and who for the most part prey on other blacks when they do, have, in fact, less excuse than their ancestors. Why should we feel more sympathy for them? Why should we marshal the prestige and resources of black organizations to plead their cases? Why should we encourage the media to play up their images and their names?

Instead, we would do better to try somehow to glorify the alternative to crime—the people who, against all odds, work hard and reject the lure of easy money and the thrill of violence to marry, raise families, and build their communities.

Truth is, they still comprise the majority of black people. But looking at the apparent priorities of the media and the supposedly representative black organizations, you'd never know it. They insist on confusing the oppressed with the depraved, but oppression does not have to mean depravity, and, until recently, in the black community it never did.

18

GLAMOROUS GANGSTERS

The best thing gangs could do for peace and justice is to disband.

Recently Wayne Capers, thirty-one, formerly a member of the Crips street gang in Los Angeles, was shot dead by rival Bloods while sitting on a bench in Denker Park. A stray bullet also claimed the life of King Clark, seventy-three, as he sat in his living room preparing for a Bible study class. In the aftermath of the shootings, city authorities shut down the park for a week, then shortened its hours during a cooling-off period to protect area residents. Possibly related gang incidents punctuated succeeding days. The *Los Angeles Times* later reported that "to return normalcy to a neighborhood of people who have been looking over their shoulders since the shootings, the area Crips are sponsoring a block party in the park today, with free food."

Meanwhile, in Kansas City, Missouri, Benjamin Chavis, the recently-ousted head of the National Association for the Advancement of Colored People lent legitimacy to the first national gang summit, a conclave of gang leaders from around the nation dubbed—apparently without intentional irony—the

"National Urban Peace and Justice Summit." After three days of secret meetings, the gang leaders issued recommendations that predictably attacked the police and called for "the immediate establishment of 500,000 jobs for at-risk youth" through government and private sector efforts. The gang leaders who have styled themselves the "true voices" of urban America, also called for repeal of anti-gang legislation and the establishment of community patrols to protect people from the police.

The people who organized the summit doubtless want the public to take it as a sign that the street gangs around the country can somehow be turned into constructive forces in their communities. Given the gangs' record of murder and depravity, why should anyone believe this? It's okay to believe in repentance, but we've got to be a little suspicious when the first thing the sinners ask is that we remove the laws and guardians against wrongdoing. The newspapers describe the gangs as "urban warriors" and they are right. Thanks to the street gangs and their elder cohorts in the drug empire, many urban neighborhoods have become war zones. The gangs could easily do something about it. They could lay down their arms. They could take responsibility for their crimes and face up to the consequences.

I'll believe that gangs can be a constructive force when they agree to organize a national effort to collect and turn in all the illegal weapons in their neighborhoods. I'll believe it when they offer to cooperate with authorities in apprehending any gang members guilty of criminal acts, especially the shootings, stabbings, and murders they have committed. I'll believe it when they issue a national statement decrying the depraved lives they have led and pleading with other young people to avoid their mistakes and give up violence.

That's what former gang member Wayne Capers had been doing in the years before his death. That's doubtless what Benjamin Chavis would like to see happen. But that's not the agenda that emerged from the gang summit. Instead, the summit appeared to increase the glamour and attractiveness of the gang life. It created the impression that the gangs and their members may hope to achieve mainstream acceptance for their rulership in the urban neighborhoods. Young people hearing about the summit weren't discouraged from violence. Instead they got new ammunition to use against the fathers and mothers, uncles, aunts, and grandparents who are trying desperately to keep them out of the gangs.

In 1967, the Office of Economic Opportunity made a grant of nearly one million dollars to the Woodlawn Organization in Chicago to work with rival Chicago gangs on a job training program. In his book "The Promised Land," Nicholas Lemann reports that "in the history of the OEO, there was no grant that was as complete a failure." Instead of reforming the gang culture, that culture overwhelmed and destroyed the program's effectiveness. We need effective answers to the disintegration of our urban neighborhoods, based on neighborhood self-government and empowerment. But we can't short-circuit the process by turning power over to the violent thugs who have been responsible for so much death and moral corruption.

The best thing the gangs could do for peace and justice is to disband. Short of that, their summit has no more credibility than the "free" food at the block party in Denker Park. It's not free at all. Wayne Capers, King Clark, and countless others paid for it with their very lives.

19

WHERE THE BUCK STARTS

We won't change the abuses until we reform the attitude that produces them.

A man called a radio talk show recently to express his anger and frustration about taxes and wasteful government spending. He was particularly upset by the scandalous savings-and-loan bailout.

At the end of his intense and angry outburst, he concluded, "I don't know why the taxpayers have to pay for this bailout. Why doesn't the government pay for it?"

If you think about that one for a moment, your involuntary chuckle should turn into a frown of dismay.

Have we really reached the point where Americans are so used to focusing on the net pay box on the paycheck that they have ceased to think of their gross income as their own? Are there taxpayers out there who believe the government has some magical source of revenue that isn't taken, directly or indirectly, out of their pockets, their labor, their economic activity?

Just because the government can take it away from us by force doesn't mean it's not ours to begin with. Yet many people are like the irate talk-show caller. They have started to refer to the "government's money" as if it doesn't belong to the people.

In this they follow the example of the bureaucrats and politicians at all levels of government who treat the taxpayers' dollar as if it were simply their own.

That's what's really disturbing about the reports of abuses in the use of official travel services. Our elected and appointed officials no longer seem to see themselves as public servants. They no longer seem to understand that any claim to special treatment they may have is a matter of public interest, not personal privilege. They no longer seem to believe that the public resources they have access to are not private fiefdoms they can use for personal gratification or advancement.

This lack of public spirit explains both the little abuses of travel and other privileges and the larger abuses of public confidence and trust that surfaced during the savings-and-loan bailout, and that fuel billions of dollars in special interest pork-barrel spending each year.

We won't change the abuses, though, until we reform the attitude that produces them. Unhappily, the trend in our thinking and practices is in the opposite direction.

These days politicians talk as if the money belongs to the government unless we can prove otherwise. That's the real logic behind the demagogic "soak the rich" tax proposals that are suddenly resurfacing in Congress.

The people making the proposals know that they won't raise additional revenue. In fact, they aren't pretending that this is the goal. Tax relief for the middle income brackets is what they promise, at the expense of the upper-income taxpayer.

The envy and resentment these proposals exploit is natural enough, but they rely on a logic that is ultimately aimed at everyone. If people who work hard enough, or are lucky enough, to realize higher incomes have no just claim to their money, on what grounds can the rest of us lay claim to what we make? If, without any other justification, government has the right to determine what each individual keeps, then we're saying that no individuals have the right to keep anything unless the government grants it to them.

The idea of a basic individual right to property that the government must respect is tossed aside in favor of a socialist understanding of property as a collective good that the government distributes according to its whim.

The "soak the rich" tax proposals are therefore a politically shrewd way of getting the mass of our people to buy into socialist logic without having to declare socialist objectives. By manipulating class jealousies, by telling us the logic applies only to the rich, contemporary demagogues mean to lure us into accepting the notion that property belongs to the government unless the government says otherwise.

By following this approach, the day will come when our paychecks won't record our net pay, they'll record our government allowance. In words, it's a small difference, but in fact it's the difference between economic slavery and economic freedom.

20

SOCIALISM AND THE STATES

*Has the California dream become the economic
equivalent of a bad LSD trip?*

President Clinton believes that the United States won't recover
economically until California turns around.

Since the state accounts for over 12 percent of the U.S. gross
national product, his view has surface plausibility. Yet when the
presidents of the twelve Federal Reserve Banks appeared before
the Senate Banking Committee not long ago, they had encouraging things to say about economic prospects everywhere in the
country except New England and California. In addition, California's woes are likely to be compounded by the Clinton Administration's proposed military base closures and cuts in defense
spending. Eight California bases are slated for closure, a move
that the state's pols say could boost its unemployment rolls by
50,000 to 80,000.

I wonder if it's just a coincidence that the two regions still
economically prostrate are also the ones that have been in the van-
guard of socialism American style. On the environment, California
has led the nation in the imposition of tough anti-pollution

standards and other regulatory measures especially burdensome to small and medium-size businesses. Like George Bush at the national level, Republican Governor Pete Wilson went along with tax increases to deal with the state government's financial bind. As one might expect, this hasn't fostered optimism in the private sector. When I visited the state recently for a speaking engagement, for the first time I can remember I heard people talking about moving out of the state. Has the California dream become the economic equivalent of a bad LSD trip?

Doubtless some people would say that a little decline in the state's population might not be so bad. Wouldn't it reduce the demand for public services? Unfortunately, if the ones who leave turn out to be mostly economic producers (scientists and engineers from the defense industry, entrepreneurs seeking a more favorable business climate) the squeeze on the public sector will only get worse. The government can't afford to choke the private sector goose too hard. After all, though the liberal strategists of class warfare want us to forget it, that's where the money really comes from.

Given the size and influence of California's congressional delegation, and the Clinton administration's ties to the Hollywood-based cultural revolution, the rest of us can't afford to ignore what goes on there. As Lenin said of politics, we may not be interested in California, but California is interested in us. People used to say the state held up a mirror in which we could see the nation's future. In that case, the future looks like an economically bankrupt welter of authoritarian paternalism, moral confusion, and multicultural decay. Things have gotten so bad that some have proposed dividing the state into two or three separate states.

Before they leap though, Californians ought to think hard, since that would mean supporting two new bureaucratic establishments. Since government spending expands to consume the tax money available, my bet is that before long each would be just as large and costly as the present one.

As California goes, so goes America. Or so the president would have us think. This time, though, California appears to be having a hard time catching up with the rest of us. Contrary to the title and basic premise of the recent movie *Falling Down*, it's not just that the state has fallen down from the economic prosperity of the '80s. It's that the weight of its subjection to and dependency on the government sector is making it hard to get up. Bill Clinton ought to consider the possibility that California's problems are the consequence of bad economic policy, not the bellwether of national recovery.

Contrary to the myths in his stump rhetoric, in most parts of the country a recovery has been under way for some time. What we really need to consider is whether the Clinton economic plan won't do for the recovery what a similar strategy of tax, spend, and regulate has already done in California, that is, turn a potentially golden promise into a broken dream.

21

The Hazards
of Health Care Reform

*The high cost of health care in part reflects the price
we are paying for bad habits.*

Something like 34 million Americans are without medical coverage, of whom 85 percent are workers or their dependents.

Americans spend more per capita on health care than any other nation—$750 billion per year, or 12 percent of our gross national product. That's expected to reach $1 trillion, or 15 percent of the GNP, by the year 2000.

No wonder politicians from both the left and the right continue to talk of reforming the health care system—despite the demise of Hillary Clinton's once vaunted plan.

Clearly, all of us should be concerned about the current state of health care provision. But let's be clear to correctly focus that concern.

In terms of its quality and sophistication, American health care is among the best in the world. Statistics don't always convey the facts, either. For example, America has one of the highest infant mortality rates of all the industrialized countries, yet our doctors have the best record in the world when it comes to saving low-birth-weight babies.

We have a higher incidence of heart disease and other cardiovascular ailments, but our medical professionals are among the leaders in bypass operations and other surgical procedures.

Part of the problem arises not from the quality of medical care, but from demographic realities and bad health habits. Higher birthrates among low income mothers mean more children at risk from the lack of information, lack of proper nutrition, and exposure to bad influences—such as smoking, alcohol, and drugs—that poor people have to deal with. Our consumption of high fat, low fiber diets means greater risk of cardiovascular and intestinal ailments. And so forth.

The high cost of health care in part reflects the price we are paying for bad habits and bad socio-economic conditions. If we convert to government financing, and don't change those realities, we simply make our problems worse.

Some of our bad habits are encouraged by the system we use to finance health care. Many existing health insurance plans make no provision for regular checkups and preventive care. The terms and deductibles are such that we actually encourage people to wait until an illness is well advanced, and more expensive to treat, before doing anything about it. That's especially true of people with marginal incomes even when they have health insurance.

The third party payment system contributes wasteful cost increases. Because those third parties—such as insurance companies or government—make most medical payments, the actual consumers of medical care don't take the same interest in the cost that they do when buying a refrigerator, an automobile, or a house. The system pushes people toward high-end medical treatment, then removes their incentive to question its cost.

Thanks to the cost effects of this sort of illogic, health insurance premiums have become employers' second-largest expense of doing business, second only to salaries. And most arguments in favor of a government-based financing system emphasize that the paperwork and bookkeeping burdens the present system entails would be reduced. Yet simply shifting the cost to government, while doing nothing to address these systemic deficiencies, would just be moving the mess around, not cleaning it up.

Proponents also cite the supposed success of the Canadian system as a recommendation to us. But Canada is a relatively homogeneous society with a small population and nothing like the massive social problems we face, especially in our urban areas. The Canadian system has also failed to curb rising medical costs, produced long waits, especially for the most critical medical procedures, and encouraged many skilled health professionals to emigrate to the United States seeking a better return for their skills.

A costly experiment in socialized medicine won't address the real deficiencies in our health financing system, some self-interested political demagogues may say. Instead, we should look to another route—one that empowers individuals and families to make the choices and take the responsibility for their health.

We should revamp the present system to put greater emphasis on preventive care and provide tangible incentives to people who practice good health. We should legislate family tax credits, including an earned income feature that will provide help to working people presently left out of the system.

Let's build a new finance system around ideas that empower people, not government.

22

PROTECTING PERKS

In Washington, there is honor among thieves.

I don't know why everyone is so surprised at reports of scandalous corruption at the highest levels of our government—such as the late-great congressional check bouncing calumny.

Congress has been overdrawing its account with the people of this country for years, confidently expecting taxpayers to cover for them. So 134 of them decided to do the same thing with their personal checkbooks. They wrote thousands of bad checks, some for several thousand dollars. No penalties were assessed; no fees or interest paid. It was just another little congressional perk.

I'll wager that many of us have, at some time or another, received an insufficient funds notice from our bank. Maybe we were caught by an error in our addition, or a check that didn't clear quite as quickly as we expected. Whatever the explanation, the bank didn't care. They charged a penalty, and in many cases, so did the recipients.

The notice was a shocker, that left in its wake a strong feeling of guilt and inadequacy, at least until the matter was cleared up.

Of course, there are people who write bad checks purposely, with no intention of covering them, and for as long as they can get away with it. Until now we called them criminals. In the future we will probably call them "the honorable" such and so, and treat them with the respect due their high offices.

On second thought, we won't be able to call all the congressional offenders by name because leaders from both sides of the congressional aisle agreed to slough over the whole issue.

We shouldn't be surprised. Some time ago when the House members raised their salaries against the wishes of their constituents, the party leaders agreed to a conspiracy to protect members from adverse voter reaction. This is more of the same.

Perhaps this bipartisan complicity arises from the fact that illicit check writing is just the tip of the iceberg of congressional privileges. Washington wags say there are similar unpaid balances at congressional restaurants.

Sometime back, I'm told some of Ralph Nader's people tried to get a full accounting of the formal and informal perks people in Congress enjoy. They got nowhere.

I would say it's high time for a full investigation. The public has the right to know about every perk and privilege hiding out in the corridor of congressional power. After all, directly or indirectly, we foot their bill. Truth to tell, the bill goes into the billions.

Why? Because the rubber check mentality extends to the appropriations process, where individual congressmen and senators treat federal outlays like their personal patronage accounts, getting and spending taxpayers' money with no thought except for the special interests who fatten their campaign war chests.

Take Senator Robert Byrd, West Virginia Democrat, as one example. Using his position as chairman of the Senate Appropriations Committee, he managed to get $137.3 million—out of a nationwide budget of $418 million—for highway demonstration projects in West Virginia. His other pork barrel trophies include a $60 million wildlife habitat and training center that will house a gymnasium and an indoor swimming pool (apparently the wildlife in West Virginia need a good workout), the transfer of the FBI identification center to West Virginia at a cost of $185 million, restoration of a private theater complex in Huntington at a cost to us of $4.5 million, and an estimated forty-seven percent of the fiscal 1992 national highway demonstration project funds.

Just as the bipartisan congressional leadership covered for the House's bad check specialists, so the other members of the Senate have refused to stand against Mr. Byrd's egregious raids on the public treasury. Indeed, they did him special honor not long ago, unveiling bronze plaques designating the leadership's offices the "Robert C. Byrd Rooms."

So in Washington, there is honor among thieves, for theft is what it amounts to when public funds are used without compelling public interest justification. People who care about the future of representative, democratic self-government in America should be deeply concerned by this spectacle.

When officials create for themselves special enclaves of privilege, when they comply with a conspiracy of silence and obfuscation to hide and protect their privileges, when they abuse public confidence to strengthen their narrow political or personal interests, at the public's expense, they have crossed the Rubicon that separates the sincere representatives of our interests from those who wish simply to dominate and bleed us dry.

23

MAKING THE WORST OF BAD SITUATIONS

The "don't ask, don't tell" policy institutionalizes moral confusion and hypocrisy.

The Clinton administration's record of broken promises, leftist radicalism, and general incompetence has kept Mr. Clinton's popularity down and Republican spirits soaring. Ah, the exhilaration of having a good, big political target to aim at, who obligingly provides fresh evidence every week—in some weeks almost every day—that the Democratic Party's leadership is out of touch with America's feelings and values.

His stand on homosexual rights, his radically leftist appointees, and his not very well disguised proposals to raid middle-class America's wallets, doubtless have the Republican polls and media consultants sharpening their sixty-second spots for a real political bloodletting during the '96 election. Republicans can certainly be forgiven if they are tempted to think that this is a situation in which worse is better, and therefore secretly cheer the administration's policy errors and excesses.

Thinking only of the nation's best interests, though, it may be that worse is just that. For example, Mr. Clinton spins fine rhetoric about military preparedness during a visit to Pearl Harbor while pursuing a radical homosexual rights policy for our armed forces that threatens to undermine morale, the real bedrock of military strength.

The "don't ask, don't tell" policy may be the best bureaucratic compromise under the circumstances, but it institutionalizes moral confusion and hypocrisy. This will do permanent damage to the respect for institutional integrity that long ago displaced personal charisma as the source of command authority for military forces. Whatever the intention, it makes deceit and dissembling official requirements of the code of military conduct.

Gone forever is the image of the soldier as a blunt, plainspoken individual, who knows that lying is just another form of cowardice. What soldiers will be truthful when the first order is that they lie to themselves? How much respect will they retain for the civilian authorities that impose this lie upon them? The ones with the most integrity will be the most chagrined, the most likely to leave rather than accept such personal corruption. If the honest soldiers quit, what kind will we have left?

On another front, the administration may also be planning to alter the mission statement of the American military, to institutionalize subordinate participation in U.N. military efforts, such as the ones conducted in Somalia or Bosnia. Some want to make training for such efforts part of the curriculum for U.S. troops, and to designate certain U.S. units to be held in readiness for U.N. operations. The proposals sound innocuous enough, until we begin to think about their real-life implications.

When U.S. forces acting under U.N. command get into serious trouble, who should come to their rescue? If the U.S. government won't automatically commit additional forces in such situations, how much confidence will American troops have that they won't be left stranded in a hostile situation?

If the U.S. government will automatically come to their aid, does this mean that non-American U.N. commanders will have the ability to embroil the United States in conflicts we might otherwise choose to avoid? In conducting themselves in such circumstances, will U.S. officers and troops be able to count on the backing of U.S. officials and public figures to defend their actions, or will they be left to the tender mercies of international opinion? And when they are called upon to die, will it be for the American people that they sacrifice, or the motley conglomeration of oligarchs and petty tyrants that still makes up the U.N. majority?

Since America assumed the responsibilities of global leadership, military life has become increasingly complex. But U.S. troops knew that they should be true to their country, true to their oath, and true to themselves. Now it seems they will be ordered to lie to themselves, while holding themselves in readiness to serve international masters whose commands may or may not reflect the values of their country. For the sake of domestic social engineering and what could very well be prematurely utopian internationalism, we are endangering the character and spirit of our military forces. In this area at least, the Clinton administration could have an adverse impact that will continue to develop for years after it is gone, and that will prove hard to undo.

24

BRUTE FORCE

A government hardened against the fate of its citizens is a danger to us all.

Even if we give Attorney General Janet Reno and her colleagues the benefit of every doubt, it's hard to avoid concluding that their tragic incompetence contributed decisively to the deaths that occurred in Waco, Texas.

Let's assume that, based on intelligence from their listening devices or other sources, officials concluded that David Koresh was becoming increasingly volatile and dangerous. Let's assume that, as Miss Reno has suggested, he was abusing the children under his control. If officials felt the continuation of the standoff posed unacceptable risks to the lives of the innocent people (that is, especially the children) Mr. Koresh held in his power, they were justified in the decision to take action to forestall violence against them.

Here's where the questions arise. If their objective was to stop or prevent violence to the children, was this reflected in their plan of attack? Apparently, they told Mr. Koresh beforehand that they were going to use force. They bombarded the compound with tear gas for several hours. They escalated the pressure, but left the situation entirely under his control. Apparently, they thought that this use of force would put so much psychological pressure on Mr. Koresh that he would surrender, or that it would terrify his followers enough to turn them against him. This thinking might have made sense if they thought they were dealing with a rational person, susceptible to the normal range of emotional responses.

But given Mr. Koresh's behavior over the past several weeks, Miss Reno and her colleagues must have seen what was patently obvious to the rest of us. David Koresh was a madman, or at the very least a fanatic who had to be treated like a madman. In either case, any decision to provoke him should have been accompanied by contingency plans to cope with the consequences if he reacted irrationally.

In fact, prudence dictated that any use of force be predicated on the worst case assumption that he would react irrationally. In that case, the first priority should have been to do everything possible to safeguard the lives of the children involved and wrest control of the situation from him quickly.

Logically, this goal would dictate a plan aimed at distracting Mr. Koresh momentarily while the government moved in a force large enough to take control of the situation. The timing for such a plan should have been measured in minutes, not hours, since once the government moved every minute Mr. Koresh was left in control was a moment in which innocent lives could be lost. Instead, the attorney general decided to play mind games with a madman. The administration plan left Mr. Koresh in control of the compound for several hours after the action commenced.

No matter what excuses the attorney general tries to invent now, the plan she approved didn't aim at safeguarding the lives of the children under Mr. Koresh's control. In fact, the plan appears to have contained no provision whatever to minimize the danger his irrational reactions might pose to the children, or others being held in his power against their will. She and her colleagues acted with incompetent disregard for the innocent lives at stake. They acted like people who wanted to get things over with, no matter what the cost. They acted like bureaucrats, more concerned for their jobs and their public image than for the value of human life.

The Congress and the public have an obligation to insist on a full investigation of this incident, and that the people in charge be held accountable for their decisions. As a civilized nation, we cannot afford to leave a precedent like this unchallenged. Knowing the bureaucratic mentality, it would make it easier for officials in some future standoff to believe they can cavalierly sacrifice lives in order to cut short an embarrassing situation. A government thus hardened against the fate of its citizens is itself a danger to us all.

25

WEALTHY POLITICIANS VS. CITIZEN STATESMEN

Our politicians should put their trust in the people.

In a gesture as phony as the solution it proposes, the Senate voted recently to bar its members from accepting speaking fees in order to supplement their salaries.

Senator Christopher Dodd, a Connecticut Democrat and sponsor of the amendment containing the ban, declared that "the time has come to rid this institution of the perception that the men and women who serve in this body have a price tag on them."

Of course, if members of the Senate have a price tag on them, any outside earnings will do nothing to remove it. Senators who could be bought before the ban will still be for sale after it passes.

But instead of openly, they will be forced underground, into elaborate subterfuges that will more easily escape the attention and reaction of the voters.

In fact, efforts to prevent financially pressed senators from augmenting income openly will simply increase their financial distress, making them riper targets for covert payoffs.

The ban on outside earnings will therefore be a self-defeating sham. Its supporters argue, however, that the Senate, like the House of Representatives, should be brought into line with executive branch policies against honoraria.

But is it proper to assume that members of Congress are merely employees of the government? These days they generally act as if they are, but that's because they have forgotten their true constitutional role, which is to represent the people.

Unlike appointed bureaucrats, the check on their conduct isn't an elaborate structure of rules and regulations. It's periodic elections, that give constituents a chance to scrutinize their conduct and turn them out of office if they have performed badly.

Suggestions such as an honoraria ban reflect the tendency of our supposed representatives to think of themselves as part of the permanent government, rather than as citizen representatives whose salaries are meant to facilitate their work, not compensate them for it. The distinction is significant.

Unfortunately, proponents of the ban have forgotten this distinction, too. They are supporting a measure that will actually make it harder for ordinary citizens to turn aside from other walks of life for a time in order to spend a few years in the service of their fellow countrymen.

With measures such as this they are, step by step, turning Congress into a preserve for the wealthy, an oligarchic clique for the moneyed few. How else can we explain the fact that the so-called reform proposals limit outside earnings to 15 percent of their salaries, but place no limit on the unearned income (interest income, etc.) that generally accrues to the wealthy?

Why do they assume that senators will be more prone to dishonest influence if they must work for a living? Is that really more corrupting than large investments in sectors or activities that may need political protection?

Why do they assume that it's all right if senators live off their financial assets, but corrupting if they benefit from accrued political assets, i.e., an occasional financial boost from events organized by those who support their views?

Rather than trusting laws and regulations, our politicians should put their trust in the people. Let politicians earn their income from whatever sources they please, with only one requirement—that every last dollar of that income be declared fully as to its source.

In the arena of political competition, that information should be sufficient to allow challengers to expose the legislators who are in the pay of particular interests, and defeat them if voters think it matters.

I think the same principle applies to the problem of campaign finance reform. It's hard to believe that incumbents in Congress will ever pass a campaign reform law that doesn't make it more difficult for them to be defeated.

Campaign finance reform is just an excuse for more incumbency protection. Instead of pursuing this unnatural myth, let's have open books and widely published notices where sources of campaign finance for candidates and political action committees will be immediately and publicly declared.

That way voters will know who's been bought and by whom. Armed with that information, the rest is—and should be—up to us.

26

FOREIGN AID EXCEPTIONS

Everyone has their favorite candidate for the program we love to hate.

Foreign aid is everybody's favorite whipping boy, which makes you wonder how it has managed to survive for so long, even during Washington's rare and illusory periods of budget growth deceleration. One reason may be that we all have our exceptions to the general anti-foreign aid bias. Foreign aid is wasteful, except when we're helping fledgling democracies in Eastern Europe or working to stave off economic collapse in the states of the former Soviet Union.

Foreign aid is highly objectionable, except for our loan guarantees to Israel, or the aid we give to Egypt as part of the Middle East peace process. From Poland to Lesotho, from Bangladesh to El Salvador, everyone has their favorite candidate for the program we love to hate. In order to get aid for the countries they like, legislators end up tolerating an idea that in general neither they nor their constituents care for.

Recently President Clinton gave Liberty medals to Frederick W. de Klerk and Nelson Mandela, South African leaders who had just reached a historic agreement paving the way for multiracial elections and the first major step toward a democratic government that now represents all the people of South Africa. Mr. Clinton pledged American support for their continuing effort. He alluded to the fact that the injustices of apartheid had left many blacks in South Africa with inferior housing and inadequate schools. He promised to urge his fellow leaders at the Group of Seven summit to give special attention to these needs.

Making allowances for the politically motivated effort to shore up his blotchy image among black leaders in the liberal establishment, Mr. Clinton's gesture toward South Africa's future bespeaks a laudable intention. Nothing is more important to the future of the African Continent than the success of representative government in South Africa. A stable and thriving Southern Africa will energize the continent's richest potential, providing the platform from which to promote real progress in Zaire and the Congo, at the continent's heart.

I confess that South Africa would be high on my list of favorite exceptions to the general antipathy toward foreign aid. I'm tempted to cheer Bill Clinton on as he urges the world to pass the hat for the victims of apartheid. But then I realize what a disservice we will do to South Africa's people, particularly her black people, if we continue to think of them as victims. Now they are nation builders, who need something more than charity and gestures from the international community.

The agreement in South Africa means that the negative policy of anti-apartheid rhetoric and gestures can no longer masquerade as an adequate agenda for the international community. Nations who undertook to withdraw their presence and investment in South Africa as part of the anti-apartheid campaign must now think about how they can be part of the positive process of building a stable, prosperous democratic future there. This was always the real challenge.

It would be a mistake, though, to look on this as a foreign aid process for the victims of apartheid. That approach looks backward toward South Africa's cruel past. Look at South Africa in terms of its many strengths, and seek to build on those strengths. Among South Africa's blacks there are already many people ready to go as managers, entrepreneurs, skilled producers. They need financial, as well as technical support in their efforts to become more integrated with the modern international economy. Standard foreign aid projects, funneling money government-to-government through inefficient bureaucracies and political networks, will end up consuming millions while wasting South Africa's most valuable resource.

South Africa needs venture capital, the kind you get from corporations rather than governments. The people who spent so much time and effort getting investors to pull out of South Africa need to organize just as massively for them to go back in. I wonder, though, if that will happen. In many countries, when black majorities finally gained their rightful power, international investors backed off, or made deals that exploited the continent's natural resources without helping to develop its indigenous economic infrastructure. To avoid this in South Africa, an anti-apartheid platform clearly won't do anymore.

Unfortunately, because America's black leaders defined the issue only in a negative way, the transition to a positive goal may prove difficult.

27

SAFETY VALVE FOR TV

The media moguls will howl, but parents who care will be grateful.

Unable or unwilling to do anything very effective to help curb real crime and violence on our streets, federal legislators are turning their attention to the realm of fictional mayhem.

One Texas Democrat offered a bill some time ago that would impose fines or threaten the licenses of broadcasters who let excessive violence pollute the airwaves. Representative Edward Markey introduced another, shrewdly dubbed the "Parental Empowerment and Television Violence Reduction Act," that targets manufacturers. Any set larger than 13 inches would have to include a chip with special electronic circuitry to allow parents to block violent programming. The bill already needs amending though, since broadcasters would have to add a characteristic warning to their program signals for the chip to work.

Only the most obtuse libertarians would contend that broadcasters have no responsibility toward public safety and decency. There would be a problem, though, deciding what constitutes offensive violence. We might all agree that the mayhem on a cop show like *Renegade* needs to be curtailed, but what about

Murder, She Wrote or *Top Cop,* or the local news shows? The *Star Trek* universe isn't notorious for mindless or offensive violence. Yet recently I noticed a warning about violent content prior to an episode of *Star Trek: Deep Space Nine.*

The objection to offensive violence surely isn't an objection to the depiction of any violent act. The classic film *High Noon* for instance, culminates in a violent showdown between the lawman played by Gary Cooper and the outlaw who has sworn to take his life. But the movie isn't about violence; it's about courage, and the need to stand for what is right even when threatened by violence. A society can't afford to produce people who are simply incapable of dealing with the reality of violence, a population of physical cowards.

Programs that depict violence in the context of portraying the struggles of will and conscience that people must endure as they deal with it are so far from being offensive that no society that wishes to maintain itself could afford to be without them. Of course, in this age of specialization, we might believe that only professional police and soldiers need this kind of education. But if the rest of us become sheep, what's to keep our guard dogs from acting like wolves? A free people can't afford to let some folks specialize in the virtues that permit them to dominate all the rest.

This issue is so profound that it forced the ancient Greek philosopher Plato to invent a new system of politics—his famous *Republic*—to deal with it. That's not exactly the kind of thinking broadcasters are trained to do. The Markey bill avoids putting them under this burden. Instead, it strengthens the hand of parents, who must deal with it already in any case, even if they aren't as wise as Plato.

By making it mandatory for the whole industry, the bill will actually help to reduce the cost of implementation, since electronic devices are more economically produced in massive quantities. Polls indicate that most people would be glad to pay a little extra for their sets in order to regain some control over this area of their family's life.

If there's any problem with the bill, it's that it doesn't go far enough to address the problem it's supposed to be dealing with. In the first instance, violence isn't an act, it's an attitude. When people are seen to have no more value than things, when they are portrayed or spoken of as if they are no different than insects or soap scum, hurting and killing them doesn't seem to be of much consequence. Rap songs that reduce women to sex objects encourage violence. Comedy routines that treat sex and human relations in gutter language that drains them of all meaning, encourage violence. TV shows that wallow in mindless materialism, and that encourage people to believe that sexual gratification, a fancy house or a fine suit of clothes are worth more than family, friendship or moral integrity, encourage violence.

Any system to empower parents ought to involve a ratings scheme that allows parents to deal with these things, too. The present movie rating system isn't perfect, but it helps. Something like that ought to be worked into Mr. Markey's proposal. The media moguls will howl, but parents who care will be grateful. Technology has done a lot to undermine their authority. Using technology to restore a bit of it will be welcome indeed.

28

SOME BADLY GARBLED SIN TAXES

If we want to lower medical costs, then we'll just have to regulate lifestyle choices.

Despite the fact that the Clinton health care reform plan was shot down in flames quite some time ago, the concept continues to animate any number of new tax schemes. The latest incarnation of this ruse is a proposal to levy a 25 percent tax on the sale of guns and ammunition. The logic is simple. Guns, like cigarettes, cause medical problems that lead to expensive treatment, reportedly adding $4 billion annually to the nation's health care costs. For gun control enthusiasts, this proposal has added luster, of course. But for the moment, let's leave aside the gun control aspects, and consider the implications of the medical expense argument.

Though we live in an otherwise very forgiving—not to say licentious—era, our public officials have discovered a way to restore what our preachers and ministers apparently failed to maintain: the concept of sin. The basis of the new religion, its *summum bonum*, is the health of the body. Health costs offer a tangible barometer of the overall extent of sin in this new religion. The higher the medical cost, the greater the sin. Moreover, people who sin should have to pay, since if they don't, the rest of us end up paying for them anyway. Hence the idea of levying taxes on sinful behavior.

So far so good. The problems arise when we begin to think about just which sins to tax. According to one study, for instance, the health care costs of obese people are eleven percent higher than those of thin people. If this is true, it would make sense to find ways to tax products that contribute to being overweight. Perhaps we should levy a tax based on the content of food products. Cardiovascular ailments are another major source of medical expenditures. Consuming too much sodium aggravates these ailments. So we should levy an additional tax based on the food item's sodium content.

Folks being taxed for what they eat might feel unfairly burdened, though, if we fail to go after another major cause of illness—the lack of exercise. The same study suggested that people who walk less than a half-mile per week file fourteen percent more health claims than people who walk more than 1.5 miles per week. A regular program of physical exercise can lead to dramatic positive improvements in overall health status.

It's not logical or fair to concentrate on the sins of commission, while letting sins of omission off the hook. Of course, this means passing a law that requires every citizen engage in a suitable exercise program on a regular basis, in a fashion that can be verified for enforcement purposes. Any person unable to prove they have satisfied the law's requirements would be subject to a unfitness surtax on their income tax.

In 1979, a Surgeon General's report concluded that unhealthy individual lifestyles account for many of the foremost causes of illness in our society. If we want more health, and lower medical costs, then we'll just have to regulate lifestyle choices. This time around our paternalistic government leaders are singling out guns, but the possibilities are endless. They will choke on the suggestion, but what about a tax on risky sexual behavior including a surtax on adulterers, homosexuals, and anyone who has more than one or two sex partners in a given year? Wouldn't that be a more effective way to control AIDS-related medical costs than spending additional billions looking for a cure that may not be found for years, if ever?

Before the logic of this health Neo-Puritanism goes too far, maybe you should stop and think about where you fit in. When they came for the smokers, you did nothing, since you were not a smoker. When they come for the gun owners, maybe you'll do nothing, since you are not a gun owner. But when they come for the homosexuals, the adulterers, the promiscuous singles, where will you be? And when they come for the overweight eaters of fat-laden ice cream and salt-packed junk food, will you still do nothing? But then, my friend, they will come for you, the unfit idlers, the people who don't run or swim or jog or walk. The people who do nothing.

29

GUESSING WRONG

Has chaos come again?

It appears that the only way to avoid being wrong in one's assessment of events in what used to be the Soviet Union is to refrain from commenting about them.

If you thought Mikhail Gorbachev would survive, you were wrong. Of course, if you thought he couldn't survive, you were also wrong. And whatever you may have predicted about Yeltsin has surely been proven wrong.

If you thought communism wouldn't outlive the failed hard-line coup attempt in Moscow, you were right—sort of. But if you predicted the Soviet Union would survive the communist regime, you were wrong—sort of.

The pace of events has moved so quickly that the failure of our nation's "all our eggs in one basket" approach isn't worth lamenting. The historic forces at work are so large that policy can't get much beyond the kibitzing stage anyway.

There's no guarantee even now that the apparent trend of events in the erstwhile Union of Soviet Socialist Republics and its axis of influence will continue unaltered. If it does, we can declare both the demise of communism and the disintegration of the Soviet—née Russian—empire. The concentrated, organized danger posed by the "Evil Empire" will have passed.

Then why don't we feel that the world is more secure?

Well, just take a look at Bosnia and you'll have a ready answer.

The fact is we still aren't sure yet whether the collapse of the Soviet empire and its satellite system in Eastern Europe means that freedom is blossoming or "chaos is come again." From a single, united, if often grotesque conglomeration of peoples could emerge a dozen or more separate states. Despite the talk of freedom, free enterprise and representative government, these states will be comprised of people with little or no experience with an open, competitive political system. From time immemorial they have been the subjects of some despot or other.

Just as the Russian economy bears the debilitating wounds of tyranny in every part, so do the minds and souls of people abused by centuries of tyranny. They will not master the complex realities of self-government overnight. They may not master them at all.

The Eurasian region that now emerges from the rubble of empire is larger and more complex than Europe. Beneath the thin veneer of communist repression, numerous nationalities, races, and religions dwelt more in tension than in harmony. Now that they are no longer cowed or mediated by the requirements of a strongly centralized system, these tensions could become the basis for fierce rivalries and conflicts.

These could soon produce the kind of battles and skirmishes that repeatedly ravaged Europe before the two world wars temporarily exhausted its soul and its resources.

Disintegration may produce a clutch of unstable regimes strongly inclined toward some form of despotism based upon military, religious, or nationalistic forces. Peoples with a weak democratic tradition, whose unifying passions have been repressed for too long, may prove highly susceptible to a fanatical style of demagoguery that transforms budding attempts at self-government into nightmares of collective self-abuse.

Such a scenario implies the emergence of individual dictators or gangster-style oligarchies in some of the new Eurasian republics. Russia itself may be less susceptible especially if it cements ties with the free democracies of Europe. But the Asian republics could develop along lines that reflect the continuing grip of political and religious despotism, especially in China and the Muslim world.

The prospect of chaos, aggravated and encouraged by economic collapse, has driven some Western observers to tout the need for massive Western economic aid to the emerging Eurasian region. They are deluding themselves, however, if they think that economic aid can avert these dangers. Money won't calm the cauldron of passions that may overflow now that the communist pressure cooker has given way. Though we Americans sometimes seem to have little patience for it, the years ahead may require policies as complex as the new realities we now face. We should probably applaud the idea of a politically decentralized, economically unified confederation in the region, but we shouldn't count on it. We should hope for a single security authority that controls the massive stockpile of nuclear weapons, but we shouldn't count on that, either.

Political good wishes, emergency humanitarian aid, nonmilitary technical advice and determined pursuit of an effective U.S. defense against nuclear attack—the Strategic Defense Initiative—that should cover the bases while we wait for history to lay out the ultimate costs and consequences of Eurasia's long nightmare of tyranny.

30

VISION'S PURPOSE AND PRICE

Democratic peoples have a special need for long–term goals and visions.

I was headed for lunch not long ago when I passed a man selling raffle tickets. I wasn't going to stop, until I heard the words "space education." It turned out that the prizes in the raffle were two telescopes, with proceeds going to support a project aimed at encouraging black youngsters to take an interest in space sciences and exploration.

The man selling the tickets was J. Hammond Robinson, a somewhat eccentric devotee of what he calls "space culture." He publishes a newsletter, *Space Culture Review*, and strives mightily it seems to live the future now. I ended up buying a ticket, and hoping that the idea behind his efforts would bear good fruit.

To be sure, the youth of our cities today are beset by all kinds of problems—poverty, crime, drug abuse, deteriorating families, and much more. Given these problems, it may seem absurd to believe something like space exploration could capture their imagination.

I know as well that there are some who oppose space exploration on the grounds that there are more pressing human needs to be addressed here on Earth. But I think they forget what may be the most pressing human need of all—the need for a sense of purpose and meaning in life that goes beyond this moment, and that links us with a future larger than ourselves. As long as children dream dreams inspired by that sort of meaning, they may live in poverty, but poverty never lives in them.

The same could be said about all of us, really. In the second volume of his magisterial *Democracy in America*, Alexis de Tocqueville suggests that democratic peoples have a special need for long-term goals and visions. So much about our culture focuses on the present, on immediate gratification and satisfaction, that we are inclined to forget our ties and obligations to both past and future. Yet without that sense of obligation, especially to future generations, what is there to inspire great efforts and great achievements? People who live only for today build only for today, which means they leave no lasting legacy.

A commitment to space exploration is surely not the only future-oriented project we can set for ourselves, but it's certainly one of them. It involves extending our reach into an environment indifferent to our needs, and therefore hostile to our existence. Hence the first requirement has been and remains fuller knowledge of ourselves—of our capacities and limitations. Armed with this knowledge, we improve our chances of surviving in space, and on Earth as well.

With this in mind, I hope the recently released *Stafford Report* will help re-energize America's long-term commitment to the space exploration effort. The report was issued by a governmental interagency panel, as a part of efforts to renew our space exploration initiative. The report presents four plans for humankind's future in space, including a Mars exploration project, establishment of a human outpost on the moon, and efforts to develop lunar resources in order to help meet Earth's needs.

A major flaw in the report is the failure to provide cost estimates for these ambitious plans. However much we justify the space program philosophically and emotionally, public support can't be sustained unless people are convinced that the dollars devoted to it are carefully spent. The tendency to present plans without price tags suggests a strategy that commits the public to an ambitious goal in order to hold us up for big bucks once it is too late to turn back. That looks less like a sound plan for space exploration than a high-sounding scheme for sustaining the space bureaucracy.

Those like me who value the inspiration our space program provides should insist space planners add accountants to their armies of scientists and engineers. The universe may offer infinite opportunities for new knowledge and experience, but the taxpayer's purse can't match that infinite capacity. We should keep our hopes in the heavens but our costs down to Earth.

31

TOUCHSTONE OF CONSCIENCE

*The twentieth century has truly been the valley of
the shadow of death.*

Recently, controversy flared briefly over a film on anti-Semitism being shown as part of the permanent exhibition at the U.S. Holocaust Museum. Some visitors reportedly criticized the film for asserting that anti-Semitic Christian teachings helped make it possible for Hitler to pursue his genocidal project to wipe out European Jewry. Critics asked why such sectarian propaganda should be tolerated in a museum made possible, in part, with public funds.

After reading these reports in the press, I decided to go and see for myself. I concluded that the film itself simply does not deserve the criticisms leveled against it. It presents, in a straightforward fashion, a few facts about the religiously inspired anti-Semitism that prevailed in European countries for centuries.

I did find myself wishing, though, that the filmmaker had made clear the extent to which Nazism had its spiritual roots outside the entire Judeo-Christian tradition. Hitler sought to revive the old gods, the symbols and violent ideals of Germanic paganism. He particularly relied on the pagan notion that one's duty to the fatherland in this world displaced allegiance to God as the primary moral motivation.

Yet the film rightly assumes that the success of Hitler's genocidal intentions must be considered in the context of Europe's long history of discrimination, slurs, and slanders against Jewish people, as well as the violent pogroms and expulsions that periodically decimated Jewish populations in various countries. When Nazi killers herded Jews into walled ghettos or onto trains headed for the death camps, when they burned synagogues or killed families outright in the streets, where was the spirit of militant Christian love that should have risen up against these devilish acts? Was it lulled by the hateful falsehood that the murderers of Christ were reaping what they had sowed?

Much anti-Jewish hatred and violence in Europe had its roots in the doctrine that the Jews as a whole were responsible for the death of Christ. Today, most Christians understand the error of this repugnant doctrine. They see the truth that Christ himself was Jewish, that Jews were the early apostles and disciples who planted the seeds of Christian faith. They accept the discipline of Christ's injunction to love all human beings as their brothers and sisters, children of the same God.

Unfortunately, though, for many centuries both the historical facts and the spirit of Christian love were corrupted and ignored by fallible human beings who professed to be Christians, but who followed instead a perverse spirit of hatred for all Jews. The film notes, for example, that on their way to the Crusades, Christian warriors slaughtered thousands of Jews, believing this was part of their holy mission. By calling upon that same spirit, Hitler managed to corrupt or silence the consciences of the large majority of German Christians.

On behalf of all humanity, we must feel ashamed of those who perpetrated or tolerated the Nazis' wholesale slaughter of innocents. But our purpose in remembering the Holocaust is not just a matter of shame or guilt. Today, we face many issues that are issues of conscience. When, for example, people make and heed the supposed counsels of caution in the face of atrocities in Bosnia; when they accept the taking of innocent life in the womb; when they stir up ancient prejudices in the name of biblical righteousness, how can we know who speaks with the voice of true Christian conscience and who, like Hitler, encourages and exploits its corruption?

A project such as the Holocaust Museum does not provide any easy formula for making this judgment. But it offers a touchstone of conscience to help discern the false from the true. It depicts, in grim detail, the terrible years during which a people looked into the true face of evil. If we do not forget what they saw, what they endured, perhaps we have a better chance of recognizing evil when we look upon its face again.

To be sure, in this century the victims of the Nazi-inspired Holocaust were not alone. Some part of their awful vision was shared by people in the Soviet Gulag, in the Maoist cultural revolution, in the killing fields of Cambodia and Uganda. The twentieth century has truly been "the valley of the shadow of death" for countless millions.

The Holocaust Museum allows our hearts to walk in the footsteps of some of those who fell in that valley. In this it serves no single religion or group of people. Rather, it helps to inform and purify the true voice of conscience that we all share.

32

THE HUMAN CONSCIENCE
AND JUSTICE

There is a God. And we are not Him.

At the foundation of America's great experiment in liberty are certain moral values—the values of freedom, justice, and virtue. Though we give frequent lip service to these values I sometimes wonder how serious we are about them?

I guess the test comes at critical moments when we are called upon to do something about these core principles. The real test comes when we are called upon to make judgments or accept responsibilities that actually require us to make sacrifices and bear what often turns out to be the very difficult burden, of being a free people that refuses to deny its interest in maintaining and preserving that justice which is the foundation of human freedom.

But again, I have to wonder. We do not think these kinds of things through very often. And that can create great problems.

I was forced to face this reality time after time when I served at the United Nations several years ago—particularly, when I was called upon to deal with an orchestrated hostility toward America's relationship with Israel.

Some of the countries represented in the General Assembly of the United Nations do not care for Israel very much and simply do not respect its existence. They are very vocal in their opposition to everything that Israel stands for.

I was the U.S. Ambassador to the Economic and Social Council, and yet I would have to say that I spent somewhere between 50 and 70 percent of my time dealing with our policy toward the Middle East in general and with the U.S.-Israeli relationship in particular. This was because in every environment there—whether it was a population conference, an economic conference, or an environmental conference—those critics would bring up their criticisms of the U.S. partnership with Israel.

I don't know why—maybe out of some peculiar judgments about my predilections—Jeanne Kirkpatrick, for whom I was working then, seemed to think it was a good idea to send me out as the paladin to fight these battles. And so I ended up spending a great deal of time dealing with these issues.

What I discovered was that at one level, our special relationship with Israel is not too terribly easy to defend. That level is the practical, pragmatic, entirely material level: strategic interests, sheer economics, geopolitics, what we have to gain, what we have to lose, where the oil is, where the shipping lanes are, and who we have to please.

It occurred to me that in the end, you can't sustain the argument in favor of a strong partnership with Israel solely on the basis of those considerations.

In fact, the world has an unwieldy way of changing, so that there might even be compelling geo-strategic reasons why we should actually abandon that partnership.

Folks in the State Department have a tendency to think this way, you know. They actually see our relationship with Israel as a pain in the neck—as something that interferes with our ability to deal in friendly fashion with the more numerous countries of the Arab world.

Realizing that, I was forced to consider: why sustain our unique partnership then? I came to believe that the best case that we can make is not at a geo-strategic level at all. It is at the level of our moral identity.

When we really get down to it, when push comes to shove, and we come face to face with the ultimate issues of war and peace—whether in Bosnia, Haiti, Somalia, Iraq, or Israel—all of those geo-strategic things go by the boards. If we were to go back and look at the speeches of our great presidents and statesmen in times of either crisis or opportunity, the arguments they appeal to are arguments that stir the moral sentiments of this nation, and that call upon our willingness to moral commitments, to the things that we believe are right.

It's very difficult to ask people to go out and risk their lives and die—particularly citizens of a free country—when what you're telling them is that they are risking their lives for mere materialistic considerations. At the end of the day people will not fight and die for a prosperity they will not enjoy, houses they will not live in, and material things that they will not be able to use. Of such stuff courage is not born.

Ultimately, when you deal with war and peace you deal with the moral dimension of human life.

There is an old Latin saying, "*Dulce et decorum est pro patria mori.*" It literally means, "Oh it is sweet and proper that one should die for one's country." Certainly, there is a satisfaction and glory in a life sacrificed for the sake of one's nation. There is a redeeming aspect to the grief one feels, something that allows us to be elevated and to look back upon the life lost as a life nonetheless fulfilled—because to die for one's nation is to sacrifice all for the ideals, virtues, and principles that the nation embodies.

That is a moral consideration though, not a material one.

So in the end, the most important argument we can make about war and peace is not the geopolitical one. It is not the strategic one. It is not the interest-based materialistic one. It is the moral one. For a people like ourselves, it is that understanding that will sustain us through the darkest days of war and will give to those who fight for us the heart to do so with willful courage. And you know, it is will that wins in the end in war.

So when I look at our special relationship with Israel, when I look at the international situation, I think about it a little differently than some, because in addition to all the other things we have to consider, I am always wondering what these issues look like in the light of what ought to be our standards for judging right and wrong and justice and injustice.

Perhaps that is why, these days, I am often accused of being someone who will only talk about morality. There was a young lady in New Hampshire who accused me of that. She came up to me and said: "You're the person who talks about morality all the time, aren't you? How can you *do* that" she asked, "when it is such a divisive issue? We can't agree about that."

I have to admit, I was really taken aback by this, because it struck me as a very sad commentary on the days in which we live—we are raising a generation of young people who believe that as Americans we have no ground for moral agreement.

The fact is, if we have no ground for moral agreement, then there is no basis on which we can sustain the will to prosecute war if and when we must. If we lose the moral understanding which allows us to come together for the sake of the principled goals for which we are willing to give our lives, we simply won't be able to sustain ourselves in the adversity of war, and in the face of its more gruesome challenges.

Thus, when I used to go around defending the U.S.-Israeli relationship, I always asserted that it is the moral identity between the United States and Israel that is our most important consideration. To sustain that argument of course, requires that we have an understanding of our common moral ground.

We must be clear on this: the moral principles that this nation stands on, are not principles lost in the mists of time.

They're not things we are making up as we go along. In fact, we know what they are. They were clearly articulated when the nation was founded. They have been at various reprises in our history hallowed with the blood of our patriots, and called upon by those who were living without justice. And they have been used successfully to motivate our will in war and to move our conscience in times of peace, to shape this nation's institutions in light of its better principles.

And I am grateful for that—it is one of those things I'm thankful for every day about being in America—not that this was ever a perfect country or that our people always did the right things. But at the beginning of our history, our Founders set down certain principles. Those principles are true—so that in spite of all our human frailty and weakness, in spite of the whole weight of human history which was against the quest for real justice, we have managed decade by decade through these two centuries and more of our existence to move in the direction of greater and greater respect for justice, liberty, and right.

The words of our Founders still ring down, through our history, with a grand decisiveness: "We hold these truths to be self-evident that all men are created equal, that they are endowed by their Creator with certain unalienable rights."

Everything we are, everything we claim to be as a free people is summarized in this principle. Everything depends on these words being true. If these words are not true, then our whole experiment in self-government is absurd, and has no real foundation in the human desire for justice and right.

When we have gone abroad and we have invoked the wonderful ringing hope of freedom, it is these principles, summarized in these words, that give content to our valiant fight for the rest of humankind.

So what happens if we back away from those words and sort of toss them into the dustbin of history? What happens if in our practice, we abandon them in favor of an understanding of freedom that disregards the meaning and consequence of those principles? What happens to us? Well, I think we lose our way like someone who drops his compass in the wilderness, or when the stars disappear behind the clouds on a night when you've forgotten to take a reading and your ship sails on but you know not where. Because our guiding star, our guiding principles, our essential selves would be lost, be gone.

That was one of the powerful arguments that was used during the course of the civil rights movement in the fifties and sixties. We were very conscious of the fact that if we continued to disregard our basic principles at home, those principles would lose credibility and we would lose our will in the struggle to defend them around the world.

You see, America's founding principles have certain implications. Their implication in the 19th century was that slavery was wrong—we had to do something about it. It took us a while, we struggled hard with it, cost us a terrible war and lots of bloodshed, but in the end, to reconcile ourselves with our principles we had to do away with this institution that violated them.

In the twentieth century we had again allowed an accretion to develop in the nation's life—racism and racial discrimination—and we had to deal with that too. And then along the way there were other things—how we deal with our children and how we regard the rights of women, for instance—all under the same rubric: that we must respect the basic principles of the *Declaration*.

Today we are in the midst of a crisis quieter than those others, but more deadly. Once again we are embroiled in this business of deciding if we will throw those words into the dustbin. But the *Declaration* is very clear: we are all human beings. If I get the sudden urge to walk through town killing people, according to the *Declaration*, I will have transgressed their basic rights and violated the community at large. I have no right to do that.

Now it could be that when someone asks me why I would do such a thing, I could say, "Well, these are just Jewish people and they're not human." The Nazis said that: "They're subhuman. We don't have to care about their lives. We can slaughter them.

We can exterminate them. That's our choice. Our scientific experts support this view. And all the public opinion polls back us up."

At various times throughout history some human beings met the arbitrary test of "real humanity" established by the elite and powerful, and others did not. Many of us here in America today, would not have qualified. Our lives would have meant nothing.

Clearly, our principles of conscience are vitally important. According to the *Declaration* we simply cannot disregard the humanity of others because we choose to do so. It says, not that we are all equal because we agree on it, or that we are all equal because the Constitution says so, or the Bill of Rights says so.

The *Declaration* tells us clearly where rights come from: "We hold these truths to be self-evident that all men are *created* equal, that they are endowed" not by the Constitution, or the Bill of Rights, or the Supreme Court, or anybody else, "they are endowed by their Creator."

That is so important for us to grasp. You and I do not have anything to do with it. Our will and our judgments and our choices have nothing to do with it. Our humanity and the unalienable rights attendant upon our humanity depend only upon this: the will of the Creator, God.

That puts us out of the picture. God made us human. That is it. There is no choice involved.

Sadly, that is not a very popular notion anymore. Thus, we have a movement in this country—it calls itself pro-choice. This movement is made up of people such as Stephen Douglas. He was pro-choice when it came to slavery—he didn't care if it was voted up or voted down so long as it was done by popular choice and state vote.

But according to the Declaration, we don't get to decide that kind of thing in our State Legislatures. We don't get to decide that in Congress. We don't get to decide that in the Supreme Court. And we don't get to decide that in our own personal lives—as a matter between ourselves and our doctors.

Because it is not our choice.

We have no right to violate those rights and that humanity—which come not from our choice but from the hand of God.

I'm smart enough to know that if we take the principles of the *Declaration* and toss them into the dustbin, the first people they will come for will be mine. But you may very well be next. When the powers-that-be have decided once again, that humanity is a matter of choice, then there will be no safe refuge for any of us, for human will and human ambition have proven themselves in this century to know no barriers of shame, no barriers of conscience—none whatsoever. Power armed with that shameless immorality will never cease in its thirst for innocent blood.

As a nation we really need to wake up in this regard. I don't see how we can come to the end of the twentieth century and not realize how deadly is the effect of disregarding moral principles.

That not only means Nazis at the gas chamber, it also means women in the quiet of their hearts, in their choice to respect or disrespect the humanity of their unborn children.

Whatever decisions we make, whatever votes we cast, whatever choices we determine—whether about Bosnia or Israel, about economics or politics, about life or abortion—they ought to be made in light of the history of the twentieth century where the shameless destruction of human conscience was conducted by devilish demagogues who understood how to unleash the principles of righteousness on the side of evil.

There is only one way to prevent that from happening again. That is to remember that there is a God. And we are not Him.

33

THE WANTED CHILD

We didn't know it was You.

Advocates of abortion-on-demand more often than not subscribe to the insidious slogan "every child a wanted child." They insist that it is better for children who would otherwise be born into the hardship and dangers of poverty not to be born at all.

Thus, they often publicly castigate pro-lifers as "very religious non-Christians" with "slave-master mentalities." As an issue in our political life, I believe abortion should be dealt with as a matter of civil and human rights, not religious controversy. But since abortion advocates insist on assailing the pro-life position as non-Christian, I hope I'll be forgiven if I take the space of a few paragraphs to address the issue in that context.

Christ was not a silver-spoon messiah. I was reminded of this quite recently when I heard again a spiritual that Mahalia Jackson used to sing that carries a message that abortion activists really ought to ponder.

Sweet Little Jesus Boy,
They made you be born in a manger.

Sweet little Holy Child,
They didn't know who You were.

Didn't know You'd come to save us,
Lord, to take our sins away.
Our eyes were blind,
We couldn't see,
We didn't know who You were.

Long time ago, You were born,
Born in a manger low.
Sweet Little Jesus Boy,
The world treats You mean,
Treats me mean, too.
But that's how things are down here:
We don't know who You are.

For centuries, Christians understood that the main point of the story of Christ's birth is that the seemingly poor, powerless, lowly people of the world may turn out to be the most important people of all.

That message is one reason Christianity had such appeal for the enslaved black people who might have sung this spiritual, despite the cruel hypocrisy of the so-called Christians who oppressed them. They took hope from the Christian saga of one born to be mocked, scourged and crucified, as they were, but whose destiny it was to change the world for good. This hope gave them a strong defense against the worst danger of their oppressed condition—the danger that oppression would kill their spirit, steal away every shred of their self-respect, until they accepted and believed the lie at the heart of the slave system, the one that said they were not human beings at all.

For many enslaved blacks, the Christian faith became the basis of their main defense against the moral degradation of slavery. Thanks to their faith, they could experience the depravity of the slave system without being depraved by it. This is no small achievement. It's what prevented most black people from succumbing within themselves to the spirit of violence directed against blacks during the years of slavery and Jim Crow repression.

Many of the so-called Christians who support "abortion rights" doubtless profess to be compassionate liberals, people who care about what happens to the poor and oppressed. Yet they join in a movement based on the idea that those who will be born into poverty and suffering aren't worth saving, that they are better off dead. They implicitly accept the idea that the lives of the oppressed are worthless, precisely the view Christ's story is intended to refute. When they read about the sixteen year old on a shooting spree, or the junior high student murdered for a pair of sneakers, I wonder if they see the consequences of this insidious, soul-destroying presumption? Can we have peace on our streets while we nurture violence in the womb?

In His words, in the manner of His birth, His life and His death, Christ demonstrated that every life may have value, that every life is worth saving, because the lives the world considers most dispensable may hold the key to its salvation. Christians believe that centuries ago, on the road to Bethlehem, in one such lowly unborn child, the Redeemer lived. But in His own land, they didn't know who He was.

The so-called Christians who support abortion rights should ponder this. On the altar of these supposed rights, millions of Christ-like unborn babes are being offered in sacrifice. We don't know who they are, but we let them die as if we know for sure.

It just seems as if we can't do right. Look how we treated You. But please, sir, forgive us, Lord. We didn't know it was You.

Three

STAKING A CLAIM FOR OUR DESTINY

Leadership in this country right now involves standing up and forthrightly and persuasively presenting to the American people the case of conscience—for those things we know to be right.

34

TRUE DESTINY

America's founding principles presuppose truth.

W inston Churchill was the consummate English statesman. He came at the end of the spiritual development of the English people. At the culminating crisis of their historical existence, he focused and articulated their national spirit, in a mighty effort that required an awareness of their whole history.

He had to bring that history to bear, to make his country-men feel the meaning of its spirit, which was, after all, their national soul. Unlike Churchill, the consummate American statesman must bring the future into focus. Hegel wrote that "America is the land of the future, where, in the ages that lie before us, the burden of the world's history shall be revealed."

The true American statesman must make us aware not of what we have been, not even of what we are, but of what we may become.

Churchill's individual existence had no meaning apart from the spiritual history of the English people. He could fulfill his destiny only in a way and at a time that brought to bear the full weight of that history.

Similarly, the true American statesman's individual life can have no meaning apart from the future of the United States. He must fulfill his destiny in a way and at a time that requires a clear vision of America's spiritual essence, a vision that allows her to bring to light the human future asleep in the womb of her history.

Hegel was right to see in America the revelation of the burden of the world's history. America's spiritual essence has to be universally conceived, for it is the essence of humanity the American people must articulate. Not a particular people, but the human race as such must find itself in America, for we are the New World, the world made over again to substantiate the possibility of mankind's universal good, which is true freedom.

Like Churchill, the true American statesman will have to complete a task of reflection, but it must be a task that is visionary rather than historical, one that requires the crystallization of a spirit that as yet has formal but not concrete existence. But unlike Churchill's England, the United States is still very much at the beginning of the process of forging its national identity. In its concrete form, the American spirit is still developing, the soul of the American people still being discovered.

Yet because our original principles and because our nation today embraces every kind of human being, it is hard to distinguish the discovery of our spirit from the development of the human spirit itself. We will not find what it means to be Americans unless we seek the meaning of our common humanity. We will not fulfill our destiny as a nation unless we realize how, through our experience, mankind fulfills its destiny as a united race.

Unfortunately, today the serious intellectual foundations of the idea of humanity have been neglected, discarded or consciously broken down. Who speaks today about human nature, or seeks to discover in the multifarious array of human societies the recurrent themes that mark them all as one? Who seriously contends that in the jangling diversity of human religious, ethical and moral codes there is some striving toward a universal chord that sways all human hearts and consciences? Who still believes that, beyond the visceral promptings of fellow-feeling, there is a natural logic that dictates respect for human rights, and grants legitimacy only to those forms of government based upon it?

America's founding principles presuppose the truth of all of these premises. Yet today in almost every field of inquiry and thought they are disparaged and condemned. This has been clearly evident in the anxious reaction in some quarters to Judge Clarence Thomas's reported belief in the importance of "natural rights" doctrine in interpreting our constitutional rights.

We live in an age when people preach humanism without believing in humanity, when they revel in universal love and the longing for community while rejecting the concepts and principles without which truly human affections and communities are inconceivable.

One quiet but critical advantage of the debate Judge Clarence Thomas's ascension to the Supreme Court has aroused could be the revival of an interest in America's "natural rights" tradition. By rediscovering the stake we have in a serious concept of humanity, we may yet achieve the contribution we have as a nation to realizing it.

35

SPIRITUAL HEALING

This republic was not a dream. It was a prayer.

The most important truth we can represent before a watching world, is not only the truth of God's authority and the discipline of respecting and fearing His will, but the truth of God's forgiveness and His love. His willingness to bring to every heart that opens to His grace the lightness that comes from knowing that our sins have already been forgiven is the profoundest of all notions.

Recently I was reading from a book of poetry entitled *The Soul of America*. As I read one poem after another I not only perceived the grave condition of our land, but also discerned in them the consequences that are even now emanating from that condition—particularly as it relates to our moral and spiritual life.

The question that immediately came to my mind as I concluded the small volume was, "Will America survive?" Of course, I don't mean, "Will the buildings still be here?" At this moment the ominous shadow of nuclear destruction has passed over us. Instead, I mean, "Will the great experiment in freedom that we have enjoyed for the past two hundred years endure or will it expire?"

One need not be an alarmist to recognize what was made so evident and manifest to me in that poetry: that the future of America is sorely threatened. We are faced in America today with a threat to our integrity and to the future of this nation. It is not a threat that is going to fall on us in the form of nuclear bombs. It is rather a threat that is coming into being as a result of what is happening to our hearts and souls.

We have a lot of people in our midst today who are like walking wounded in a spiritual war. Some of them have been struck dead in their spirits and yet they still walk amongst us.

And thus, there is no conception, I think, that is more necessary to America's life today than that we should heal. How do you heal a wound so many among us don't even recognize?

At the end of one of these verses, the poet conjured up an image that I thought was so devastating in its potential truth, that anyone who read it ought to be arrested and turned around. It was the image of God rocking the cradle of aborted babies, as he commands his angels to dance on the grave of America. I wish I could say that it did not strike me with a word of truth.

But just as God is a God of love and a God of mercy, so also is he a God of justice and a God of judgment. He gives rebellious peoples second chances, and third chances, and more—as Abraham discovered as he looked over the valley of Sodom. That being said, we must admit that right now in America, we must be in an Abraham moment. Surely Abraham must still be speaking to God, and asking, "If I find just fifty, will you spare them?"

The question for us then is: "Who shall the fifty be, and who shall the ten be, and who shall the one be, for the sake of whom God might spare this land, the judgment for its transgressions."

I think in order to understand that this has some relevance, outside of this communion that we share, we will have to turn back to some truths about America's history that seem always to be forgotten. To continually return and call people's attention to the great words and great truths that were spoken at the beginning is a vital task for our time. In order to go forward, we must first reach back. We must once again put before our eyes that which gives us a sense of the mission for which we as a people are going to be held accountable.

We have been, as a nation—as almost everybody is wont to say—remarkably blessed. We are rich, and powerful, and endowed with all manner of prosperity. Sundry sciences and technologies have burst upon the scene to deal with human problems and find solutions, cures, and successes the like of which we can hardly imagine. We could make the mistake of believing that was all because we were so ingenious, diligent, or wonderful.

But you know, you look back at the beginning, and what the founders of America made clear—when they stood naked of all that power, naked of even the possibility of success—we get a different perspective altogether. They were a ragtag bunch of colonialists going up against the greatest military power on the face of the earth. No one in their right mind would have put their money on George Washington. No way. Odds were long against him. And against those that followed him, longer still. When you stacked it all up, when you added it all up, when you accounted for the provisions and the money and the training and the resources, there was no way but that you would have concluded that the American army lost. And yet, with no one on their side, and with nothing in their hearts but their commitment to what they thought was right, those intrepid Founders prevailed.

But notice, afterward they did not stand up before the watching world and announce that it was their virtues, and their power, and their strength, and their goodness, that enabled their lonely cause to triumph against all odds. They looked instead to Him who is the Judge and lawmaker over all the universe. With a firm reliance upon His divine providence, they moved forward to vindicate their claim to liberty.

Those who take seriously the Biblical tradition that God is more than willing to help in a righteous cause simultaneously acknowledge that such help is not always a free good. It is a free grace. But it is not always a free good. So, He is always there when we call upon Him. But when we call upon Him, when we say, "I shall put my firm reliance in Your divine providence," we have yielded ourselves to His will, and not our own. Our Founding Fathers clearly understood that principle.

If we have achieved earthly power, if we have achieved earthly strength, if we have achieved earthly prosperity, if we have been put in a position that we can hold up before the world a shining beacon of hope, if we have had on occasion, the chance to go abroad, and join our hands with others whose hearts aspire to live in decency, and dignity, and freedom, these things certainly did not come about because of anything we did ourselves. They came about because we relied upon God's good providence.

And he did provide. Marvelously. Beyond our wildest dreams.

But if we have relied on his providence, and if we have based our identity and our sense of justice on respect for his power and his will, what do you think is liable to happen if we begin to deny his existence, reject his authority, and hold his will in contempt?

I look back on the last several decades of America's history, and I must tremble. I think that is exactly what we have been trying to do: rebel against the good providence of God.

Reading the familiar words of the *Declaration of Independence* is thus a rather sobering experience for us in these difficult days. Right in the beginning of that great document, we read, "We hold these truths to be self-evident." Now what does this tell you in a world where all the experts tell us that there is no truth, that everything is relative. How can you have a self-evident truth when all truth depends on circumstances? "We hold these truths to be self-evident, that all men are created equal." Now, I want to know how it can be that our children should understand the source of their freedom, their dignity, their human rights as stated in that *Declaration*, yet we should be told that they cannot even be taught the meaning of creation in their classrooms today.

And even more, how can it be that this sort of convoluted separation of church and state should imply the banishment of God from country? When right there at the very wellspring of our conscience and our sense of justice, it is made clear: "And that they are endowed by their Creator ..." You know, we don't think about these words enough. It is all too easy to take them as some sort of patriotic mantra. We have repeated them so often that we have taken their profound meaning for granted. But notice: "They are endowed by their Creator ..." Endowment is an act of will. Endowment is not the act of a faceless, personality-less nature-god. Endowment is the act of a God who has purposefully willed for the good of humankind. That is a gracious and benevolent power that can see the human condition and understand its needs and respond in the outpouring of grace in accord with his perfect will.

"They are endowed by their Creator with certain unalienable rights." Once again, we must pause. It is all too easy for us to gloss over the significance of that word "unalienable." In fact, today people hardly even know what it means. Unalienable—it simply means that we cannot refuse this gift. It is an offer, that we cannot refuse. Because the rights with which our God has endowed us with are rights that we do not have the choice to surrender, to destroy, to condemn, to corrupt. In exactly the same sense that an aristocrat had unalienable land that attached to his title not to his person, so we have unalienable rights that attach to our God-given nature.

If we would but think through these words and phrases, we would suddenly begin to realize how ridiculous we have become, how shallow, in our understanding of the sources of our freedom.

Clearly, this great *Declaration* is indeed a charter of liberty but it is also a statement of the authority on which our claim to freedom and dignity rests. I believe that the smallest child among us could understand the consequence of ignoring this truth. If this authority is the ground on which we stand, if this authority is that which establishes our freedom and gives it a firm foundation, then if you use your freedom in such a way as to contravene and deny that authority, do you not cut the ground out from under your claim to rights, to freedom, to dignity?

We cannot deny the authority of God lest we deny the source of that which guarantees our freedom in the eyes of men. Sadly, that is exactly what is going on today in abortion, and so many other areas. We are starting to stand up and act as if we are our own authority, that we don't have to pay attention to God. We think, "God, Creator, what's he got to do with me? I am God now and I shall choose who is human and who is not. I shall be the one to decide where the line is drawn between those whose rights can be respected and those who at any moment on my whim and will can be destroyed. So I will reach into the womb and I will rip out the innocent life of the unborn and I will cast in the way of my ambition, and my convenience, and my career, and stand up and claim this as my choice."

But if such a choice were indeed ours, then it would be the end of our right to choose. If it is our choice, we then would contravene the very authority on which all choice must rest. And with that choice our freedom ends and with that life our own lives are forfeited.

The *Declaration* offers us a ground for freedom—but not if we reject that authority from which that freedom comes. In that sense, it is not only a reminder when we turn to those first principles of our need to respect the authority of God, it is also a reminder that whatever has occurred in the course of American history, must have been part of his plan.

You know, if our Founders turned to God and relied upon his divine providence and if time and again, you can see how successful this nation has been, I think you would have to be far gone in depravity not to realize that if we enjoy the fruits then we had best be on our knees in thanks and praise of his purposes that provided them. And that is where I think, we, the people of the *Declaration*, and people of faith, and people who believe that we have been offered the saving grace of God and the blood of Jesus Christ have a special calling. Because contrary to what everyone in the media and academia tries to make us believe, the American dream is about far more than the dingy artifacts of materialism. The toys you have, the salary you make, the house you live in, this is not all that matters. I certainly do not have contempt for the fruits of our labors or the blessings of providence. But I will say we go far wrong if we mistake that for the real purpose of this land.

The American dream was not and is not a dream of materialism. It was not the desire for mere material wealth that brought so many people to give up better lives elsewhere to come to America. We forget this. In the beginning, the people who came did not come as some did later on, huddled masses. They came from fairly comfortable situations in Holland and England. They decided to commit all their goods to frail barks and go off on the stormiest ocean, to the very ends of the earth, to a wilderness where they could not even be assured that they would find the wherewithal to feed themselves. They did this for what? They tell us what they did it for. They went upon this errand in the wilderness to find a place where in the truth and freedom of their conscience they could worship Almighty God.

If we have won some material success along the way, it has been because of that earlier, prior, predominant mission—that mission which was not a materialistic, economic mission, not a mission like the Romans in search of power or glory or conquest, but a mission to seek the face of God and to rely upon his will, a mission to obey those truths that might lead us to establish, one amongst the other, a nation where we could all live in peace and brotherhood, in mutual respect, with something like the dignity that God intended.

It has taken time. We are still human beings, subject and heirs to this fallen nature. So, yes, there have been wrongs done. Those ideals set on high have not been perfectly observed. And I, the son of those who were once slaves in America, I can tell you, it was not always done with respect for his will. But I can tell you as well, that there would have been no struggle for justice, there would have been no Civil War or Emancipation Proclamation, there would have been no forward progress for those enslaved, if we had not had emblazoned at the beginning, that which calls this nation to respect the will of God and to acknowledge his authority.

At every juncture, at every time when we were called upon to face injustice, the people who successfully rallied the conscience of America didn't do it because they were rich and powerful and everybody thought they would surely prevail. They did it because they were called by God to hearken this nation to those principles that bind us to his will. To call this nation to eradicate from amongst us those things that contravene his authority and his grant of dignity to each and every one of us, from slave then toiling in the fields, to children lying asleep now in the womb. It does not matter the time, it does not matter the color. All are entitled to the same respect for their human dignity—not out of the goodness of our human heart, but out of the goodness of God's mighty will.

That is the conscience of America. I think that what behooves us now as we face the disintegration that has resulted from the loss of the conscience, is that we must in every way we can, call this nation back to those principles that bind us to God's authority.

The one thing that strikes me as I look at all the problems we are faced with today is that once we have recaptured the sense that we must call people back to the principles of the *Declaration*, and that in doing so we call them back to God and to God's relationship to America, we still have something left to do. Those of us who are the savor of the salt, and those who are the leaven in the loaf, we will have to take the challenge of cultural renewal personally. Because there is no way that this nation is going to reclaim its spirit, reclaim its proper destiny.

That is the reason I think it is so important we realize today that whatever goes on in the way of politics, organization, and all the things that people talk about, the messes that we make as we try to straighten out the messes that we make, there is really only one true and sure way to revive the spirit and reclaim the destiny of America. That is to seek the face of God—so that he might look upon our prayers and heal our land. This republic was not a dream. It was a prayer.

So, I call on you today, as Americans, because our creed calls us to God, as Christians, because our faith moves us to live in his love and his will—let us stand up whether we know or not what the final outcome may be, let us stand up and do all that we can, in our prayers and in our faith and in our lives, to bring this nation back to where God says it was intended to be.

The hour is late—but it is not *too* late. We can still live in God's promise of freedom, equality, and justice. If we are willing but to fall down upon our knees and cry out—if we request that in accord with his mercy he grant to us the boon of bringing back the spirit of justice to a land that has long known the blessings of his will. It is not impossible for us. Because nothing is impossible for the God on whom we rely.

Take heart, then. It may indeed be true, that if we continue down the road the angels shall dance upon the grave of America. But if we are faithful, there is yet time to stave off such a fate. We may yet still attain our great destiny—if we lift up our hearts to God, those same angels shall rejoice as they rejoice in finding the lost sheep—when once again, America comes home.

If you are interested in having Alan Keyes speak to your church, organization, or special event, please contact:

interAct Speaker's Bureau
8012 Brooks Chapel Road
Suite 243
Brentwood, Tennessee 37027
Telephone: 800-370-9932
Fax: 615-370-9939